MW01124739

STABILITY
OF THE
Soul WITHIN
THE HEART
OF THE
Father

*Finding Stability in Life despite
One's Circumstances*

TOMMY SHAUGHNESSY

WESTBOW
P R E S S®
A DIVISION OF THOMAS NELSON
& ZONDERVAN

Scripture quotations are from The Holy Bible, English Standard Version® (ESV®), copyright © 2001 by Crossway, a publishing ministry of Good News Publishers. Used by permission. All rights reserved.

Scripture quotations taken from the New American Standard Bible®, Copyright © 1960, 1962, 1963, 1968, 1971, 1972, 1973, 1975, 1977, 1995 by The Lockman Foundation. Used by permission. (www.Lockman.org)

WestBow Press books may be ordered through booksellers or by contacting:

WestBow Press
A Division of Thomas Nelson & Zondervan
1663 Liberty Drive
Bloomington, IN 47403
www.westbowpress.com
1 (866) 928-1240

Because of the dynamic nature of the Internet, any web addresses or links contained in this book may have changed since publication and may no longer be valid. The views expressed in this work are solely those of the author and do not necessarily reflect the views of the publisher, and the publisher hereby disclaims any responsibility for them.

Any people depicted in stock imagery provided by Thinkstock are models, and such images are being used for illustrative purposes only. Certain stock imagery © Thinkstock.

ISBN: 978-1-5127-1391-6 (sc)
ISBN: 978-1-5127-1392-3 (hc)
ISBN: 978-1-5127-1390-9 (e)

Library of Congress Control Number: 2015915691

Print information available on the last page.

WestBow Press rev. date: 09/28/2015

Contents

Introduction

The moment a person becomes a Christian, they are baptized into the death of Christ and raised unto newness of life by the glory of the Father. The new believer becomes one spirit with Christ (1 Corinthians 6:17), thus now entering into the life of the Son and therefore entering into the life of the Trinity. However, very few modern-day Christians seem to know and understand these eternal truths. As a result, many believers today are blown to and fro by the winds of adversity and never find stability for their souls. The natural tendency of the heart is to look for peace and comfort from the world and life's circumstances. Sadly, mankind does not know its proper worth and will never find rest in the land of the living. Therefore, the only option remaining for the immaterial soul is to look elsewhere, namely, to God himself.

The spiritual stability of the human soul is found only in the heart of God through the proper foundations of the means of grace. The goal and aim of this book is to strengthen the foundations of a believer's life, thus leading to the soul's stability. The approach taken is very similar to that of the Apostle Paul, who wrote a vast majority of the New Testament. Paul oftentimes begins with theology about God and then transitions to practical application in the later portions of his letters. For example, the first three chapters of Ephesians are dedicated to theology regarding the eternal plan of redemption set into motion through Christ

(Ephesians 1:3–13), to being saved by grace through faith (2:8–10), to the mystery that has been hidden for ages and is now being revealed by God's manifold wisdom (3:1–13). The purpose of these chapters is to teach us more about who God is and who we are as children of God in light of that knowledge. Only then does Paul later make the transition to practical application: "I therefore, a prisoner for the Lord, urge you to walk in a manner worthy of the calling to which you have been called" (4:1).

The art of understanding the theological points allows the believer to have the eyes of his heart enlightened (1:18), thus enabling him to see the beauty and majesty of the glory of God (which is the external emanation and beauty of God's internal nature). In turn, the more a believer sees the glory of God unveiled through Scripture, the more he will be changed and transformed into Christlikeness (2 Corinthians 3:18). In other words, the more a believer understands and knows God intimately, the more that person will become like God through the transforming power of the Spirit. Biblically, God has so wisely designed that change is to begin internally—not externally. The more the believer understands the love that God has for him "and to know the love of Christ that surpasses knowledge," the more he can be transformed into the fullness of God—"that you may be filled with all the fullness of God" (Ephesians 3:19), thus finding spiritual stability for the soul despite external circumstances.

The design of this book follows the same pattern of Paul's epistles. The first half concentrates on essential foundational knowledge of God that leads to practical application in the second half. The second half focuses entirely on applying this knowledge through the means of grace which consists of the Word of God, praying, meditation, and other various means of grace. Properly defining these means of grace allows the believer to properly apply these means in their life. Taking these steps will establish a stronger foundation in an individual's life, which will ultimately lead to the stability of the soul in the heart of God—not the external world.

To walk with God in this world is to have the very life of God infused into the soul. That same life which flows richly between the majestic Trinity: the Father of mercies, the Son of righteousness, and the Spirit of life. One day with the majestic three is better than a thousand elsewhere. The delights of this life miserably fail to compare to that which is in the Lord. To walk with God is to have the soul firmly secure within the heart of God. The believer no longer experiences life on his own; rather, he is given a keen sense and awareness of God's presence. The soul is now given eyes to see the Lord at work within him, through him, and around him. Everything in life takes on a whole new meaning and perspective as that Christian begins to experience the life of God through these means in his everyday affairs. As a result, the soul finds its proper resting place in God himself, thus finding spiritual stability.

The path to finding such a life is found by delving deeper into the heart of God, depending, of course, on how strong and established the foundations of Christianity are in a believer's life. So let us embark on this journey by taking a deeper look at various attributes of God, the cross—the signet of his glory, the newness of life, the battle with indwelling sin, and the means of grace. In doing so, may the soul find stability within the heart of God—rather than the external world.

CHAPTER 1

Knowledge of the Holy One

The knowledge of the Holy One can be marvelous and splendid to some, yet at that same time, devastating and terrifying to others. The knowledge of God's holiness is one of the most crucial and defining elements of a Christian's life. Through this knowledge comes an intimate understanding of God, for the believer must be striving for holiness, without which no one will see the Lord (Hebrews 12:14). God's holiness comprises who he is, establishes what he does and why he does it. Through this knowledge, the believer may strengthen the foundation of his life and forsake all else for the pursuit of something more glorious.

A Vision for Life

Many saints throughout the Bible saw glimpses of God's holiness and found their lives changed forever. They were never able to return to what their lives were before and, for the most part, they never wanted to return to those old ways. The moment they saw and understood God's holiness from the heart, whether by external visions or internal understandings imparted by the Spirit, the Lord's holiness became their guiding vision and the pursuit of their lives. The things of this life became a mere afterthought as they endeavored for deeper understanding and knowledge of the Holy One.

David, one of the most notable and respected saints of the Old Testament, had a deep internal understanding of God that drove and compelled his life. Though he himself never had a vision like the apostle John (Revelations 4:1–11), or the prophet Isaiah (Isaiah 6:1–6), who saw the Lord adorned in the attire of holiness, majesty, and sitting upon his throne; David did indeed see what they saw, yet by an entirely different means. Through ever-constant meditation upon the Scriptures (cf. Psalm. 19; 119), he gained an unrivaled internal understanding of God and his ways:

> One thing have I asked of the Lord, that will I seek after: that I may dwell in the house of the Lord all the days of my life, to gaze upon the beauty of the Lord and to inquire in his temple. (Psalm 27:4)

The means by which David gained knowledge of the Holy One may have been different from Isaiah or John; nonetheless, the end result was the same. David lived a life in which he was driven to learn more about the Holy One, he was zealously driven to dwell in his house and gaze upon his beauty for all time.

Paul is another magnificent man who was blessed to see a glimpse of the Holy One. This vision drove him, like David, to seek God with all of his heart. Even so, Paul's experience was much different from David's—or Isaiah's, for that matter—as he required a much more direct approach:

> At midday, O king, I saw on the way a light from heaven, brighter than the sun, that shone

around me and those who journeyed with me. And
when we had all fallen to the ground, I heard a
voice saying to me in the Hebrew language, 'Saul,
Saul, why are you persecuting me? It is hard for
you to kick against the goads.' And I said, 'Who
are you, Lord?' And the Lord said, 'I am Jesus
whom you are persecuting. But rise and stand
upon your feet, for I have appeared to you for this
purpose, to appoint you as a servant and witness
to the things in which you have seen me and to
those in which I will appear to you, delivering
you from your people and from the Gentiles—to
whom I am sending you to open their eyes, so that
they may turn from darkness to light and from
the power of Satan to God, that they may receive
forgiveness of sins and a place among those who
are sanctified by faith in me.'(Acts 26:13–18)

Paul's glimpse of the Holy One was so overwhelming and
marvelous that the light he saw appeared "brighter than the sun"
(v. 13), and forced both him and his companions to the ground.
In his testimony, he said, "we had all fallen to the ground" (v.
14). Paul's will was broken and so overwhelmed by the majesty
of the Lord that when Christ spoke to him, all he could do was
acknowledge him as Lord, saying, "who are you, Lord?" (v. 15).
Paul was unaware of the identity of the one to whom he was
speaking, yet the sight of Christ's glory brought Paul to his knees.
The effects of that day forever changed his life as he turned from
being a murderer and a persecutor of the church (1 Timothy 1:14),
to becoming one of the greatest saints to walk this earth. He was
even used by God to write a vast majority of the books compiled
in the New Testament.

A question then arises: what did David, Isaiah, John, and Paul
see that drove them to abandon everything and live radically for

the glory of God? What knowledge of the Holy One did they gain that forever changed their lives? Such questions warrant thorough inquiry, yet I am afraid the task of accurately portraying God's holiness is immense and goes beyond our understanding. Most spend a lifetime seeking knowledge and a deeper understanding of God's holiness because of its eternal properties; however, they only scratch the surface. Our natural limitations prevent our fully fathoming such eternal truths; nonetheless, through the words of Isaiah, we will embark on this journey.

Holy, Holy, Holy is the Lord Almighty

> In the year that King Uzziah died I saw the Lord sitting upon a throne, high and lifted up; and the train of his robe filled the temple. Above him stood the seraphim. Each had six wings: with two he covered his face, and with two he covered his feet, and with two he flew. And one called to another and said: "Holy, holy, holy is the LORD of hosts; the whole earth is full of his glory!" And the foundations of the thresholds shook at the voice of him who called, and the house was filled with smoke. And I said: "Woe is me! For I am lost; for I am a man of unclean lips, and I dwell in the midst of a people of unclean lips; for my eyes have seen the King, the LORD of hosts!" (Isaiah 6:1–5)

The prophet Isaiah received one of the most blessed revelations in the entirety of Scripture, which enabled him to look upon the Lord himself sitting upon his throne in heaven. Isaiah was considered to be a righteous man in his time, yet the sight of the Lord broke him as he cried out, "Woe is me!" for, as he recounted, "my eyes have seen the King" (v. 5). I believe Isaiah not only saw the majesty of the Lord, but he also gained a heart knowledge of who God was as he heard the angelic host crying out to one another, "Holy, holy, holy is the LORD of hosts; the whole earth is full of his glory" (v. 3). That expression of praise reveals a vast amount about God's internal composition. However, to understand it from Isaiah's perspective, requires a familiarity with Hebrew culture and its ways of emphasizing things of importance.

For instance, when wishing to emphasize or place importance upon something in the English language, the writer will often capitalize letters, set words in italics, or end sentences with exclamation points. In the Hebrew language the speakers and writers used repetition as their means of assigning importance or for emphasis. A classic example of this repetition would be Jesus, in the Sermon on the Mount, expressing the importance of salvation using three different examples in sequential order, as found in Matthew 7:12–21. A more familiar example would be Jesus' repeated usage of the words "Truly, truly, I say to you" throughout the gospel of John; this convention placed double importance on what he would say next.

So for the angelic host to cry out three times, "Holy, holy, holy," reveals the immense importance placed upon the holiness of God. No other attribute of God is emphasized as much throughout the Scriptures, for the same pattern is repeated elsewhere in a similar vision: "Holy, holy, holy, is the Lord God Almighty, who was and is and is to come!" (Revelation 4:8).

Holiness does not simply have one particular meaning. Through its biblical usage, it can mean *purity, transcendence,* and *separation.* God's holiness comprises the very core properties of his being and intertwines with his attributes. Holiness and his attributes are intricately connected in every way. By his moral perfections, he shows himself to be holy:

> But the LORD of hosts is exalted in justice, and
> the Holy God shows himself holy in righteousness.
> (Isaiah 5:16)

The word *righteousness* can mean "right conduct." To put it simply, God shows himself holy by his attributes. In other words, God is holy at his core, and everything about him, including his character, is defined by holiness. Moreover, because of that link, his attributes or virtues, embody a transcendent quality defined by perfection, namely, an eternal quality utterly distinct and separated from this world that remains pure in every way.

The truths of God's holy character has significant meaning because God is described as "the fountain of life" (Psalm 36:9), meaning that all three members of the Trinity are life themselves. As the Father has life in himself, the Son likewise shares this quality (John 5:26), as does the Spirit of life (Romans 8:2). The Godhead or the Trinity is the fountain of life because the divine nature consists of life. This quality can be seen all throughout the Scriptures, but one place in particular is 1 John 5:13, which says: "I write these things to you who believe in the name of the Son of God that you may know that you have eternal life." The "name of the Son of God" means the entirety and totality of Christ's character, so for a person to believe in his name is also to say he trusts and delights in the divine nature (Hebrews 1:3). Believing on Christ's name ushers in eternal life to the human soul: "that you may have eternal life" (1 John 5:13).

This quality can be more clearly seen in Isaiah 6:3 as the angelic host cries out, "Holy, holy, holy is the LORD of hosts." This verse distinctly indicates that God's holiness is the center of his being. As a result, the "whole earth is full of his glory!" which means that *life* is the result of God being holy. The earth is formed and given life for the purpose of being "full of his glory." In other words, the earth is full of God's glory because it physically shows and emanates God's glorious character. Therefore, holiness can be said to be the vital link of life, for holiness is the chief property that flows into all of God's attributes.

Another way of understanding what holiness is and how it comprises the nature of God is to understand its counterpart— *Sin*. Sin, which is the complete opposite of holiness, represents death, chaos, and imperfection that threatens everything for which holiness stands. In the end, sin and death must be destroyed, for if left unchecked it would compromise everything for which God stands. God's justice and wrath are the means by which sin or sinful beings are destroyed for the preservation of life. It would be as if someone discovered a way to destroy the sun and had a bent disposition to carry out his discovery. For the preservation of life and the well-being of every living thing on the earth, creation or rather mankind would rise up to end this threat by preventing it entirely. The same idea can be carried over to God's moral excellency—which is holy at its core and from it flows life as we know it, whether spiritual or physical.

The nature of God's love is another good illustration. For instance, human love is flawed in every way with its conditional natural limitations. Human love comes and goes like the wind because of its conditional nature—which is a self-seeking nature. In other words, natural human love is always seeking its own best interest and will only give based on the principle of receiving something in return of equal or greater value; which is why it is conditional in nature. If an individual is investing time or energy into something or someone, that person is doing so in the hopes of receiving something in return, whether it is emotional intimacy, acceptance, belonging, friendship, joy, purpose, and so forth.

Certainly the same cannot be said of God's love. Divine love is holy in nature; its very nature and quality is eternally superior and distinct in every way. For starters, divine love is *unconditional* in nature, meaning it will dispense every resource for the sake of another without seeking anything in return and will continue to do so regardless of the results. Divine love is distinct in the sense that it's only known and seen within the being of God or rather the majestic Trinity. In general, godly love will unconditionally seek the joy and well-being of everyone and everything, whether it's a single individual or, in our case, the entirety of mankind.

Divine love is also transcendent and superior in relation to human love in its eternal proportions that cannot be measured or contemplated. Eternal love will bear any difficulties, injuries, or faults to a limitless degree that is beyond comprehension; for an illustration, look no further than Christ bearing the weight of sin of all mankind upon the Cross. It will believe the best it possibly can as far as reason will allow; however, in the case of mankind, the Father believed in us because of his Son. Divine love will hope for the very best and hope against hope; because of the eternal plan of redemption set in motion through the Son, there is hope for mankind.

Eternal love will endure any trial, test, circumstance, or the like for the sake of another. In our case, the Son endured the weight of sin and the eternal wrath of God, so that by his wounds our souls could be healed. Eternal love has limitless, boundless, eternal resources to carry out its designs. For these reasons and more, God's love is a holy love, tis also the reason why holiness is such a marvelous, wonderful, truth about God.

Holiness and Glory

At the very center of God's heart can be found holiness and glory. Everything the Heavenly Father does stems and flows forth from these two core characteristics which are intricately connected:

> Holy, holy, holy, is the Lord of hosts; the
> whole earth is full of his glory! (Isaiah 6:3)

With holiness being defined, we can now transition to the second portion of the verse, thus making the connection between God's holiness and his glory. The first portion of the verse largely emphasized the internal nature and composition of God: "Holy, holy, holy, is the LORD of hosts." The second segment reveals the results thereof of God's being a holy God, which is "the whole earth is full of his glory." In other words, God's holiness is the totality of his divine essence which comprises the excellency of the divine nature or rather who God is. God's glory is the external emanation of those internal perfections or simply God's intrinsic beauty.

God's holiness can refer mainly to his internal composition or the compositional elements of his nature, while his glory is the emanation or manifestation of those elements. Another way to consider, it is: God's glory is the external component of his intrinsic nature. So of the angelic host to say "the whole earth is full of his glory" can also mean the entire earth is full of his *beauty*. Moreover, everything within creation itself, ranging from the stars, to mankind, to the waves crashing along the beach have God's mark upon them, thus exhibiting his glory in some way.

Bringing Everything Together for Clarity

Before progressing any further I want to help bring everything together, for I often find that so many terms can create confusion if not properly explained with clarity. The words *righteousness* and *glory* both refer to the same core truth which is the entirety of God's nature. *Glory* is more specific in regard to the external emanation of those internal attributes; *righteousness* still refers to the totality of those attributes, but more applicably to doing them, for *righteousness* can simply mean "right conduct." In regard to God, the word means—true, right, and perfect conduct.

9

To bring God's holiness into the picture and shed light and clarity as to how all of these truths come together as one, it's vital to remember that holiness and glory are intricately connected according to Isaiah 6. Therefore, if glory and righteousness refer primarily to the totality of God's intrinsic nature, then *holiness* is: the defining element and essential ingredient that makes his nature the *divine nature*. Holiness is the one distinguishing characteristic that makes and defines who he is and what makes him majestic, glorious, and beautiful in every way. Holiness, which makes God's nature what it is, flows forth into all of his attributes defining them, elevating them, and distinguishing them with the mark of eternity.

God's glory is merely the manifestation of those beautiful perfections, while righteousness similarly overlaps his glory more in relation to the action or conduct of those perfections. In either case, the terms "for his name's sake," "glory," "righteousness" and many others, at the core, these terms always refer to the entire composition of God's divine nature, or simply who he is.

Why So Many Different Terms?

In case you're wondering why so many terms are used to describe the same core meaning, it is because the Bible uses this approach to teach many principles that require repetitive teaching from different approaches. In other words, the principles that God teaches his children through his Word are of an eternal nature that is limitless in their understanding and application. The tendency of human nature is to become very familiar with various key terms or ideas. As a result, familiarity can stunt spiritual growth because the mind tends to tune out the truths already learned or heard.

For this reason many core biblical principles are repeated and emphasized extensively throughout the New Testament. Spiritual growth is typically slow and consistently progressive; God, being infinite in power, could have created the vast universe in an instant. Instead, over the course of seven days, he chose to create progressively, methodically, and consistently, which, of course, reflects his nature more than anything. Therefore, it should be of no surprise that spiritual growth or the progressive revelation of Scripture throughout the centuries follows a similar pattern. For instance, the child of God may learn that the general principle of exaltation comes through humility (Luke 14:11), nonetheless, he will learn it more extensively through studying the example of Christ (Philippians 2:6-11), thus growing deeper in an eternal principle through a different external means.

Everything for the Beauty of His Glory

Everything within creation, though tainted by the Fall, still reflects his beauty. Certainly, the varying degrees may differ; nonetheless, the image of God can still be seen in creation:

> But let him who boasts boast in this, that he understands and knows me, that I am the LORD who practices steadfast love, justice, and righteousness in the earth. For in these things I delight, declares the LORD. (Jeremiah 9:24)

The whole earth is full of God's glory (Isaiah 6:3), because he is always at work within the earth practicing his steadfast love, justice, and righteousness. If God shows himself holy by righteousness (Isaiah 5:16), then the earth is a marvelous representation of the beauty of God's holiness for his righteousness can be seen everywhere. The rain falls on the just and the unjust; his mercies are rich and new every single morning. Mercy is simply one of the many manifestations of God's love upon mankind. The

Lord is always at work within the world for the display and beauty of his divine perfections. The earth and all of creation reflects the beauty of God's majestic nature through his eternal love, mercy, goodness, and so forth. Revealing God's majestic nature is the reason for everything God does. Everything that he creates, everything in which he is presently at work, and the end purpose of all things is for the display of the beauty of the divine nature:

> For from him and through him and to him
> are all things. To him be glory forever. Amen.
> (Romans 11:36)

According to this verse, everything that has ever been created or ever will be is ultimately from God: "For from him." He is the source of life; therefore, everything that comes "from him," is presently sustained by him "through him," and the end purpose of all things comes back to him—"to him are all things"—for the singular purpose of his glory: "...to him be glory forever." All things within creation...whether angelic or human—serve the purpose of bringing him glory. Even a lily flower serves this same purpose by reflecting the beauty of God's wisdom. Everything that God has ever done, is presently doing, or ever will accomplish is for the purpose of the emanation of his glory. Even demonic spirits and wicked men will ultimately bring glory to God as he shows forth his justice when they become objects of wrath (Romans 9).

It is the foundational principle of who he is and why he does what he does. In other words, questions regarding why did God create mankind, Satan, and the third of the heavenly host—knowing exactly what would take place? More specifically, that the human race in its entirety, Satan, and a third of the heavenly host—would commit treason and rebel against him? Why does he interact with mankind in ways throughout the Scriptures that give the appearance he doesn't know what may happen? Yet we know that he knows all things (Psalm 139:1-6) and nothing that happens is a surprise to him. The principles of knowing and understanding God's internal composition provide a foundational framework for answering some of these various questions... yet only in part. Some mysteries are purposefully left to God and God alone (Deuteronomy 29:29). However, these examples still provide a foundational basis for knowing God and diving deeper into his heart.

Beholding the Work of Glory

An incredible and marvelous truth is to know that God works everything together for the beauty of his divine perfections. It's quite another to see these realities firsthand through the eyes of faith. Know that every circumstance in life from the simplest occurrences of everyday life to the wind breezing along fields of flowers to the crashing of the waves along the beach shore, or even to the setting of the sun displays the beauty of God's majestic heart.

A simple day at the park can be like watching a movie for the eyes of a Christian, for the believer does not see the world as the natural man does. The world may simply see kids playing soccer at the park or couples having romantic picnics with one another, but the gracious heart of the believer sees the majestic Trinity showering people with love and mercy. They see children exhibiting reflections of God's nature through determination, creativity, skill, discipline, teamwork, and more importantly, they see their Heavenly Father's smiling as he dispenses undeserving mercy stemming from his eternal love.

To see as God sees is a marvelous gift that transcends all else in this life. The soul is given life by the Spirit of life and rides the waves of faith into the very heart of the Father; forever caught in the life eternal that flows between the royal Trinity. Some believers are blessed to see and experience this quality of life which transcends meaning itself. As believers... The Father, through the Spirit, draws our hearts to the beauty and glory of his Son, and the more we draw closer to his Son, the more our hearts are in awe of our Heavenly Father as we see his eternal plan of redemption set in motion through his Son.

The heart of the Father becomes more plainly manifest as we see he was willing to give up his one and only begotten Son, all for the purpose of loving us, redeeming us, and calling us his own (Romans 8:32). In doing so, we also learn that, as a token of his love, the Father sent us his Spirit with whom we walk and fellowship every single day. Each time we pray, the Holy Spirit is right there enabling us to pray, and in times of darkness when we cannot find the strength or the words to pray, he is right there praying for us and interceding on our behalf (8:26,27). Forever present, he is the one who comforts us in all of our afflictions, confirming in our hearts the love of the Son. Though the Son is now ascended to glory and is sitting at the right hand of the Father (Hebrews 1:3), he, by his Spirit, testifies in our hearts that we are his, he is ours (Romans 8:16), and that he will never leave us nor forsake us (Hebrews 13:5).

Glorious Perfection Open to All

Sadly, many will never comprehend or ever attain to any understanding of who God is and what it is truly like to walk with him. 'Tis not an irrational or illogical concept based on man-made knowledge; rather, it is true heart knowledge based on real fellowship and real conversation with God through prayer that is founded and predicated upon his Word. The reality is that most will never attain or ever experience the life of God because they either do not know him or they are more concerned and in love with the world around them.

Walking with God and experiencing the life of the Trinity is not reserved alone for the spiritual elite: this relationship is open to anyone who earnestly wishes to know him and seek him. If the desire of your heart is to know him, walk with him, and find stability and life of the soul in him alone and not the world, then you are already on your way to Christian perfection. The perfection of the Christian does not consist in a perfect external performance. If that were the case, then the religious Jews of Christ's day would have attained it; however, they fell utterly short. In the eyes of the Father—*Christian perfection is the sincere and earnest desire of the heart to know the Son and to become more like the Son.*

As that desire begins to grow and grow, the love of God becomes more of a reigning principle within the heart, which will mold and transform one's external practice. However, attaining perfection all begins with seeking the life of God through knowing the Son. In other words, the simple desire to learn more about God through reading the Bible and seeking him through prayer will ultimately result in a changed life. In desiring his glorious perfection, the born-again believer has the opportunity to walk with the majestic Three, which invariably brings a smile to the Father.

Unfortunately, most believers never learn or ever experience this perfection—not because it's difficult or that it's unimaginable. On the contrary, most believers simply do not want to experience his perfection because they erroneously think greater delight and fulfillment can be found in the material world around them. It's not a matter of how or difficulty; rather, it is simply a matter of choice and desire. No Christian will ever find a command or a duty contained within Scripture that God himself doesn't enable us to do. If he requires a task of any of his children: like walking with him, knowing him, and loving him with all of their hearts, he will most certainly provide the means to do accomplish it. Therefore, attaining perfection is not a matter of difficulty, rather one of choice and desire.

Perfection at Work Inside of Us

'Tis such a delight and a magnificent joy to see God at work in the world surrounding us. However, it's quite something else entirely to know and to see him at work inside of us:

> For it is God who works in you, both to will
> and work for his good pleasure. (Philippians 2:13)

'Tis the sovereign pleasure of God himself to be at work within our hearts, both conforming and molding us into the image of his Son (Romans 8:30). As God delights in practicing steadfast love, justice, and righteousness in the earth (Jeremiah 9:24), he, in a like manner, delights in fashioning and conditioning our souls unto perfection. As he works in us, he causes us to desire that which is his holy and glorious "will." As we hold out those desires through our activities, or his "work," he conveys it to completion, which also results in the joy of his own heart. That is to say, God drives the very desires of our hearts, if in fact we are walking with him. In conjunction, any activity or external practice that we may do, as a result thereof—is actually God himself through us. The more we know about God and who he is, the more we grow into the idea and understanding that the "God who works in us" is a profound mystery greater than the universe itself.

The sovereign King works in everything and brings all things together for the joy and pleasure of his own beautiful perfections. Another way of understanding it is to say God delights in working all things together for the *purpose of life and the display of his beauty.* As wonderful and glorious as that may be, it's something else entirely to think that it's the sovereign pleasure and joy of God's own heart to work in us *the perfection of life and the display of eternal beauty,* for we know that God works in all things, including his children.

Wisdom Leading to Perfection

It is a marvelous and breathtaking truth that the Lord would be working eternity upon our souls, but without having an understanding of this truth, how can it be fully appreciated? How can this truth bring the soul who does not grasp it closer to God's heart? Other questions that are most assuredly arising from the former truths include: what work is God doing specifically inside my heart? What does his work look like in life?

Innumerable truths and realities of the work God is doing in our hearts exists, but the one truth that encompasses them comprehensively is his divine wisdom. The wisdom of God is the driving engine behind all of his glorious attributes and the way by which they are externally and perfectly emanated to the watching world. Divine wisdom takes the purest means to achieve the perfect ends, which is the manifestation of God's divine nature.

Consequently, God has chosen his church to become the means through which his manifold wisdom works for all to see his glory (Ephesians 3:10). In other words, it could be stated that those who know God or his saints have eternal value because it's through them that God's wisdom works to display his glory. In short, God is at work inside of his saints perfecting them to righteousness. Through believers, his glorious perfections are emanated for all to see.

How Shall We Respond?

Even those who walked with God before us, including David, Isaiah, John, Paul, and so many others, lived centuries apart from one another, yet they all had one particular thing in common. They all possessed an intimate knowledge of the Holy One that caused them to live in reverent fear, awe, and trust of God. This intimate knowledge is properly called the "fear of the Lord" (Proverbs

9:10). However, don't let the title or expression deceive you. In one sense, it literally does mean a fear of God; nevertheless, only a certain population knows him in that way:

> And they went into Capernaum, and immediately on the Sabbath he entered the synagogue and was teaching. And they were astonished at his teaching, for he taught them as one who had authority and not as the scribes. And immediately there was in their synagogue a man with an unclean spirit. And he cried out, "What have you to do with us, Jesus of Nazareth? Have you come to destroy us? I know who you are—the Holy One of God." But Jesus rebuked him, saying, "Be silent, and come out of him!" And the unclean spirit, convulsing him and crying out with a loud voice, came out of him. (Mark 1:21-26)

Unclean spirits or demons know exactly who Christ is as illustrated by the words: "… Have you come to destroy us? I know who you are—the Holy One of God" (v. 24). The demons understand who he is and are rightfully terrified; they *literally fear God.* "And the unclean spirit, convulsing him and crying out with a loud voice, came out of him" (v. 26). Demons only know God by his power: "Be silent, and come out of him!" (v. 25). They do not know him or fear him like the holy angels or saints do. Those who truly know God know him by two distinct elements; one of those elements is most assuredly his power. However, knowing God's power does not tell you *who he is.* God's power is meant to highlight and point toward God's character:

The fear of the LORD is the beginning of wisdom, and the knowledge of the Holy One is insight. (Proverbs 9:10)

Knowledge of the Holy One produces a proper fear of the Lord. Both sections of the verse are inseparably linked, for "the fear of the Lord" is the origin of wisdom because it is the knowledge of his attributes that opens the doorway to obtaining wisdom. In other words, knowing God's character enables a proper fear of God because that fear is based upon a genuine love for God. This kind of fear consists of reverential trust, awe, and adoration that resides in the heart of any saint that truly knows him, which is derived from truly loving him.

The fear that fallen angels have of God is a fear based on a hatred for God and from experiencing his absolute power. They fear God because they hate him, but not because they know him or wish to know him. There are two fears of God: 1) one is based upon knowing from his power, and 2) the other is based on knowing his power and his character combined together which produces a genuine love of God for who he is. Knowing and seeing how beautiful and glorious God is—namely, the beauty of his love, the glory of his holiness, the tenderness of his grace, the riches of his kindness, and so many more attributes is the foundation of this reverential fear.

These attributes move a heart ever closer to God, loving him all the more and trusting him even more. These things produce a genuine fear of the Lord that is more fearful of disappointing him, dishonoring him, and grieving his heart more than anything. Yes, there is a knowledge and a fear of his power, but for those who know him, it is like eternally being caught in the eye of a magnificent storm. It is to be forever caught in awe of the might and splendor of his power, yet eternally secure in the eye of the storm, which is the very heart of God.

Dear Heavenly Father, thank you for who you are, all that you are, and all that you continue to do. From all eternity past, you have dwelt in eternal delight and everlasting love that flows between the Father, the Son, and the Spirit. To the amazing three in One, thank you for revealing who you are and for bestowing such gifts of grace upon our hearts. I pray Father, take us deeper into the very depths of your heart until we find ourselves swimming in an ocean of love and everlasting delight. May the light of eternity forever guide us and bring us closer to Thee, Amen.

CHAPTER 2

The Love of the Eternal Trinity

When the general public thinks of a good movie, they usually envision it as having a happy ending with an end to all conflict. The main characters are generally the heroes of some great ordeal who usually end up living in a land happily ever after. In comparison to the world in which we live called *reality*, that scenario sounds like a great escape. After all, the trials and hardships that come with this life certainly make such a utopian world very appealing. I think for most people, this idea would be called "heaven." Certainly, heaven truly does exist and is such a place of eternal beauty that we cannot fully comprehend. But before earth, heaven, or even the universe existed, something better already existed eternity.

Inevitably, the question of who made God or where did eternity come from is always mentioned. Here's a staggering thought to that question: if we use the reasoning of some people that God *must have been created* or have come from somewhere, then logically the creator of God must have been created as well! After all, we all know that something doesn't come from nothing. The only problem with that logic is the endless series of sources, creating things with no apparent origin. Therefore, *something* has to come from *something;* nothing, simply pops up out of the blue. So God's being eternal is the perfect solution because he is an origin without beginning or ending. Oh, and because God's Word says so, therefore, case closed.

If such a world or a place called eternity has always been and always will be, then what has an eternal God been doing for all of eternity in eternity?

The Blessed Trinity

The triune God, or the Father, the Son, and the Holy Spirit, as we know them (or simply the Trinity), have always indwelt and inhabited eternity (Isaiah 57:15). Within this blessed realm or sphere, God has dwelt in perfect harmony and fellowship within himself. Having fellowship within himself means the Father has always eternally known, loved, and delighted in perfect fellowship with his Son. The Son, likewise, has always eternally loved his Father; the evidence thereof is shown in the Cross of Calvary in his willingness to lay down his own life in obedience to his Father's command—all for the sake of his Father's name. Eternity is a realm without beginning or end; it's a place where God's glorious virtues reign supreme in unfathomable splendor. Eternity is a world without measure unto its beauty and radiance of God's eternal love.

Contained in the Word of God are hints and glimpses of these wonderful eternal truths. These truths tell of a better world—a world where the glorious Trinity is forever caught interacting with one another in eternal delight and fellowship. The Father himself, from the depths of his soul, takes eternal delight in his Son (Isaiah 42:1); Whom he has known and loved for all of eternity (Luke 10:22, John 3:35). The Son, likewise, dearly loves his Father and has been with him before the beginning of time (John 1:1). The heart of the Son is most clearly seen in his high priestly prayer in

John 17, as the Son intercedes for the disciples or those who would believe through the Word. The love and dear affection the Son has for his Father is beautifully on display for all to see in this chapter.

The Son not only shares the same nature or divine essence as the Father, but he is also the radiance of his glory (Hebrews 1:3). Therefore, the glory of the Son seen at his transfiguration or upon his throne (Isaiah 6) is also the same glory he has always had with his Father in eternity past (John 17:5). In other words, the Father, the Son, and the Spirit are all one because God is one (Deuteronomy 6:4). Everything that the Father does is also in unison with the Son and the Spirit. Even when Jesus took upon the form of a man and restricted the usage of his own divinity, he was not alone; for both the Father and the Spirit were with him (Matthew 3:16, John 16:32).

So even on earth, Jesus was still in constant fellowship within the triune God. Astonishingly enough, any interaction of the Trinity we see within Scripture is something they have been doing for all eternity. That is sacrificially serving one another in a fountain of divine love that overflows into rivers of eternal joy.

The Overflow of Divine Love

It could be said that all of creation and the world in which we live is an overflow of that divine love being expressed to the Son. All of creation was made by the Son and *for the Son* (Colossians 1:16). Yep, that includes you and me! Naturally the thought or question of if God is perfect and dwells in perfect love and harmony within himself, why did he make the universe? The truth is that he did not need to; rather, he *wanted* to as an expression of his love to the Son. Another way to look at it is that because God's attributes are eternal and require an external disposition, they are without limitations in their expressions. In other words,

23

the Father's love being expressed to his Son is infinite and without measure, and creation is the overflow of that love being conveyed.

With that thought being explained, I believe that is simply the beginning of a magnificent and wonderful truth—that all of creation being an overflow of God's eternal love also means we are forever caught in the wonderful life of the Trinity. Meaning, our eternal purpose, and existence are to have fellowship with God and to delight forever in the life of the triune God. To know that my one duty in life is to know God and enjoy his presence for all eternity shouldn't even be considered a duty; but rather a privilege of swimming in the infinite fountain of joy of whom God is (Psalm 16:11). In an ironic fashion, one of my duties is to delight and to enjoy the life of God for all eternity.

The Duty of Glory

In fact, this mandate was charged to mankind from the beginning of time. When God created the earth and formed Adam from the dust of the ground, he had this purpose in mind (Genesis 1:26, 27). This purpose, though, is not limited to man, but applies to all of creation. Everything in existence, including the angels, was created for his glory (Romans 11:36). It was the theme of the angel's song at the creation of the world (Job 38:4-7). This theme can be seen throughout all of Scripture. Our greatest delight and joy is *in* the glory of God, not outside of it, for we "… rejoice in the hope of the glory of God" (Romans 5:2).

If the glory of God is also the emanation of his character and who he is, then our greatest joy in life is from delighting in his glory, which is to say we find joy and comfort in who God is and what he does. It is to say that God is the fountain of life (Psalm 36:9), and our greatest joy is found *in him* because he *is life*. So God's eternally loving me from the foundation of the world brings sheer delight and hope to my soul; it is also the equivalent of saying my heart rejoices in God's glory because it is the shining forth of God's beautiful character.

The Fall of the Heavens

It's nearly unthinkable to imagine that in a moment in eternity past, God, who is already perfect and has no need of us, would create us to have fellowship within the Trinity and rejoice in his everlasting glory for all time. It's an even more startling thought to imagine that anyone would willingly turn down a life of endless joy with the Lord. However, that rejection is exactly what came to pass, and the one who first lead this rebellion is someone who had it all:

> You were the signet of perfection, full of wisdom and perfect in beauty. You were in Eden, the garden of God; every precious stone was your covering, sardius, topaz, and diamond, beryl, onyx, and jasper, sapphire, emerald, and carbuncle; and crafted in gold were your settings and your engravings. On the day that you were created they were prepared. You were an anointed guardian cherub. I placed you; you were on the holy mountain of God; in the midst of the stones of fire you walked. You were blameless in your ways from the day you were created, till unrighteousness was found in you. In the abundance of your trade you were filled with violence in your midst, and you sinned; so I cast you as a profane thing from the mountain of God, and I destroyed you, O guardian cherub, from the midst of the stones of fire. (Ezekiel 28:12-16)

This revelation may come as a surprise, but this Scripture refers to Satan before he fell into darkness. He was considered to be "the signet of perfection," the marking herald of all creation. His fall is a classic version of a tragedy when considering who he was and what he has now become by choice. Lucifer, along with a third of the angelic host, corrupted their hearts and waged war in heaven for the right to reign. They traded their perfect, sinless nature for sin, which defiled their hearts and actually led them to believe they could win a war against God. They were soundly defeated and cast out of heaven (Revelation 12:3-9). However, this rebellion was not limited to the fallen angels. In his fall, Lucifer was also able to enlist all of mankind to rebel with him.

The Fall of Man

After his rebellion, Satan and his fallen angels were cast down to the earth (Revelation 12:9). He set his eyes on Adam and Eve with the objective to turn them against God. His objective was not as overt as one might think. Imagine a once magnificent civilization beautiful in every way with peace and love as the hallmarks of this society. Standing in the center of this beautiful city is like watching the morning sunrise from the New Zealand countryside, beautiful and splendid in every way imaginable; however, somehow through one man's malevolent decision, that beautiful civilization came to a crumbling end.

Yet that imagining is exactly what happened, for Adam and Eve were given dominion over the whole earth (Genesis 1:28), and the couple dwelt with God in perfect paradise in the garden of Eden. What many dream of and hope for was once a reality, but it all came tumbling down the moment Adam and Eve ate from the forbidden tree. Satan tempted Eve to eat from the tree, convincing her she would not die and would be like the Most High (Genesis 3:3-5). Sadly, Adam was with her the whole time and made no attempt to intervene on her behalf (3:6); rather, he allowed his wife to be deceived by that serpent, while he knew exactly what he was doing (1 Timothy 2:13, 14). In a moment of pride like the Devil (Isaiah 14:13, 14), Adam, wanting to establish his own reign, brought to an end what was once a perfect paradise.

Much of the world in which we live and see today is like standing in the ruins of a once beautiful and magnificent civilization. Traces and remnants of that once beautiful world still remain—the stars, the beaches, the morning sunrises, and the evening sunsets. However the remaining beauty is simply a pale shadow in comparison to what it once was. Mankind once enjoyed complete dominion over the earth, but now the earth has dominion over man. In spite of as advanced as mankind has become, people are still slaves bound to the inevitable variables of this world. Outside of a divine miracle, we are left to our own facilities which ultimately cannot save us from death. Indeed, Adam's decision caused a ripple effect that has echoed throughout the entire universe, including mankind. However, it wasn't as if Adam acted alone, for through that one decision, all of mankind is also held responsible for what happened:

> Therefore, just as sin came into the world through one man, and death through sin, and so death spread to all men because all sinned. (Romans 5:12)

Like father, like son. We may not have physically been present in the garden, but in the same way, we died with Christ on the Cross (Romans 6:4), or in how the Levites gave tithes to Melchizedek through Abraham, even though their order was not around yet (Hebrews 7:9, 10), we all sinned against God through Adam in the same way. Furthermore, based on the character of God, we know specifically because of his attribute of justice that we stand guilty of sinning against a Holy God. All throughout Scripture, we see

God' holding mankind accountable for sin (Isaiah 24:5, 6; Psalm 14:2, 3; Romans 3:23); therefore, we must be *responsible* for sin for that accountability to even make sense.

God's justice dictates that he will not take action or execute judgment until the crime or action has taken place. For example, God knew what Satan and a third of the angelic host would do, and he knew what mankind would do, yet he created man anyway. God's holy justice is perfect in every way; however, our human sense of justice would say to prevent the crime before it ever took place. In a world with sin setting the standard for everything, then yes, stepping in and preventing the deed would have made sense, but God's ways are perfect, and his ways are not our own (Isaiah 55:8, 9).

Sadly, no one knew or had any idea how devastating one decision could or would really be. On the surface level, the person reading Genesis 3 may conclude that all of mankind fell for eating fruit from a tree. However, the Fall goes so much deeper than that. The external action may hold been a mere deed of eating fruit, but to God, the internal motive is every bit as significant as the external action (1 Samuel 16:7). Therefore, just as Satan rebelled in pride against God's sovereign reign, mankind, in a like manner, also did the same.

The Descent into Darkness

Unfortunately, in that rebellion we didn't simply lose access to the Garden of Eden; rather, we lost everything, including God himself. For when God said to Adam, "but of the tree of knowledge of good and evil you shall not eat, for in the day that you eat of it you shall surely die" (Genesis 2:17), Adam did not die physically right away. Adam did die spiritually, and so died mankind right along with him (Ephesians 2:1). In other words, God's Spirit departed from Adam and Eve. As a result, mankind lost access to God, and the universe fell into darkness, which was only the beginning, for all of creation was subjected to futility and thus affected as well (Romans 8:20). Death also entered into the world and has since been an adversary mankind has never been able to conquer (5:12). Moreover, death has also entered into the heart, for divine love was once the guiding principle in our souls. As a result, with the absence of God's Spirit, every man's heart has collapsed within himself, enabling the sin principle to enslave him (John 8:44). Thus, all mankind has become children of wrath (Ephesians 2:3).

It would seem almost hopeless for man at this point: every person's heart being a slave of sin, death knocking at the door of every moment of our life, Satan's enslaving us and having dominion over the world (2 Corinthians 4:4). Yet another variable still remains that supersedes the rest: Because we have all sinned against God, are born with a sinful nature, and presently sin against him, we have all earned the rights of becoming recipients of God's justice. All of mankind alike have become children of wrath (Ephesians 2:3), meaning God's eternal wrath is now fixed on us. To add the icing on top of the cake, the standard of being perfect and being reflections of God's glory still stands, "for all have sinned and fall short of the glory of God" (Romans 3:23). Man falls short of God's perfect standards because humanity can no longer have fellowship with God as they formerly did. The Spirit of God, which once dwelled within the hearts of man, enabled him to see and behold his glory. Namely, the divine love of God was the chief principle guiding and regulating every man's heart. Just as love is the summation of the law (Romans 13:10), it's also who God is (1 John 4:8). Without this divine principle, we fall short of God's glory and are utterly incapable of fulfilling the law of being perfect. The list of obstacles standing between us and being in God's presence is overwhelming to say the least. As it stands, we have utterly no hope of defeating sin or death, so what chance do we have of overcoming the wrath of the Almighty?

A Plan for Hope

In light of these truths, mankind, which used to be the center of light among all of creation, now stands in utter darkness with no hope over the horizon. The only possible way of restoration and reconciliation before God is that of a divine miracle. However, in spite of all that we have done, all that we are going to do, and every obstacle that stands in our way, God, in his loving mercy, does exactly that. For even when God was pronouncing judgment upon Satan for the fall, man was given a slight glimpse of hope:

> I will put enmity between you and the woman, and between your offspring and her offspring; he shall bruise your head and you shall bruise his heel. (Genesis 3:15)

Many have come to call this the preaching of the "first gospel" and with that, the first sign of hope for mankind. The "he" to whom God is referring is none other than the second member of the Trinity, the Son of God. For, "he shall bruise your head" is a declaration of victory for the Son against Satan through the cross. Even as God is proclaiming judgment upon Adam and Eve for their actions, the Lord infuses judgment with grace and revealing his plan to restore mankind to himself. For God the Father himself already had a plan in place before the world ever existed:

> Blessed be the God and Father of our Lord Jesus Christ, who has blessed us in Christ with every spiritual blessing in the heavenly places, even as he chose us in him before the foundation of the world, that we should be holy and blameless before him. (Ephesians 1:3-4)

Ephesians 1:3 through 14 outlines the plan of redemption designed by God the Father (vv. 3-6), carried out by the Son (vv. 7-12), and secured by the Spirit (vv. 13, 14). The first part is taking place in eternity past—"before the foundation of the world" long before the universe ever existed. The reason why this is so amazing is because God, in his infinite wisdom, decided of his own accord "that we should be holy and blameless before him," meaning that despite the fall, sin, death, Satan, our constant daily rebellion, and his own justice-demanding nature; that nothing would stand between himself and us—not even ourselves. Everything that happens within creation is ultimately serving the overall objective of uniting man to God himself, or rather the love of the Triune God.

God's Justice

Yet in order for that unification to happen, many things had to take place. Above them all God's eternal justice must be satisfied, meaning the price of blood must be paid in order for there to be forgiveness of sins (Hebrews 9:22). With God's wrath being the execution of his justice, his wrath must be poured out for justice to be served, and the fact that God is of an eternal nature necessitates his wrath to be of the same substance. Nothing in all of creation could ever appease or finish an eternal sentence; experiencing the wrath of God means enduring his wrath for all time.

However, not all hope is lost, for there is One of an eternal nature who could satisfy the justice and wrath of God; although, the idea of his subjecting himself to such a destiny is almost unthinkable. It's like sacrificing the sun for the dust of the earth, or trading what is most valuable and excellent for that which is nothing. By all rights, this kind of sacrifice should never happen, i.e., trading the valuable source of life for something that is less than worthless.

The Criminal and the King

Imagine standing in the throne room of a mighty and powerful king. You stand guilty of murder, theft, aiding and abetting the enemy, and high treason. There is no hope; the only option is capital punishment. In this matter, justice must be served; death is the only proper response. The debt must be paid. Otherwise, murderers could murder without fear of punishment, thieves could steal without any worry, and order and peace would be an afterthought in the wake of chaos. In light of these truths you begin to think of your family, and the horrors of them living in such a world; all of which awakens the realities of your crimes. These truths begin to dwell in your heart as you look up at the King, ready to receive your sentence.

The King comes to his feet readying himself to pass judgment. All eyes are on the King, eagerly anticipating his words of justice. He slams the heel of his staff to the ground and proclaims the liberating words "not guilty." Everyone in the throne room is shocked and perplexed at the judgment they just heard. Some are appalled and begin to voice their objections while you, the guilty one, stand in amazement and perplexity as the events unfold. As you begin to celebrate and plan in your heart the coming days, you look over to see the magistrate approach the King.

The entire throne room begins to fall silent as the magistrate speaks "My King, you alone are the ruler of these lands, and there is no questioning of your authority. However, even you are not above the law, and the law demands that justice be served in this matter."

The King replies, "I know what the law states and requires. Fear not, for justice will be carried out."

With a look of perplexity upon his face, the magistrate poses the question, "Sire, how will justice be served if this man is set free with no punishment? The very foundations of this country will be shattered if you insist upon taking these actions."

You look across the throne room into the eyes of the King, eager to hear his explanation.

As he looks upon you, you notice a sense of sorrow within his eyes, yet present with joy. The King returns his gaze to the magistrate. "Though I do not know this individual who has chosen to live a life of rebellion and commit treason against my kingdom, I will show mercy. I will show mercy and uphold justice by taking his place for his crimes. He will inherit a place on my throne and eat with my family at the royal table. His crimes will be remembered no more, and he will live in gratitude and humility the rest of his days. I will trade my life for his—the righteous for the unrighteous—so that all may know what true love really is."

In light of this illustration, that very king who took the place of the criminal was none other than the Son of God himself, and we the criminal. The only hope for the human race was for the impossible to happen, and since there was only justice and no plan of redemption for the fallen angels (Matthew 25:41), what were the chances for the human race?

The Value of the Son

Moreover, the only means to redemption was through the Father's only begotten Son. The very Son "in whom my soul delights" brings infinite joy to the heart of the Father (Isaiah 42:1). That Son is the very image of the invisible God (Colossians 1:15), whom he has also chosen to bring glory to his name and to reign supremely over all creation (John 17:1, 2), a member of the eternal Godhead who surpasses all things in excellency and worth. Yet despite the odds, God the Father planned from eternity past to trade perfection for iniquity, the righteous for the unrighteous, and life for death, in order that one day man might be reconciled and live once again.

The Distance Between God and Creation

It is an astonishing thought to have a small glimpse of who the Son really is and to understand that he is more majestic and beautiful than our minds could possibly conceive. An even more astounding thought is that God himself within the perfect fellowship of the Trinity, would humble himself to take notice of things infinitely inferior in comparison to himself (cf. Psalm 113:6, NASB). Even the angels, as perfect and holy as they are, stand as little to nothing before a holy God, for they are creatures while he is everything (Job 4:18). In reality, the human race is insignificant in beauty when compared to the angels, the stars, and the heavens, which all declare the glory of God. David was also aware of this truth:

When I look at your heavens, the work of your fingers, the moon and the stars, which you have set in place, what is man that you are mindful of him, and the son of man that you care for him? (Psalm 8:3,4)

It is one matter that God should humble himself to take notice of creation, for he himself is of an infinitely superior nature. However, for him to take notice of mankind that he should be "mindful of him" or "that you care for him" is an even more confounding reality.

A Glimpse of the Son

The saints of old understood this truth all too well; they knew that to truly grasp this truth meant the breaking of one's soul and being humbled to the dust. It meant to know not just how great and powerful he is and man's low estate before him, but they also saw how excellent and beautiful he is in his character—especially in his disposition of undeserving mercy and grace toward creatures of darkness. Such was the reaction of Jacob: "I am not worthy of the least of all the deeds of steadfast love and all the faithfulness that you have shown to your servant" (Genesis 32:10). And that of David: "But who am I, and what is my people that we should be able thus to offer willingly?" (1 Chronicles 29:14). And I think Isaiah may have had the best glimpse of all when he saw the Lord sitting upon his throne: "Woe is me! For I am lost; for I am a man of unclean lips, and I dwell in the midst of a people of unclean lips; for my eyes have seen the King, the Lord of hosts!" (Isaiah 6:5).

The instant Isaiah laid his eyes upon the King is also the moment his heart was shattered into a million pieces. In comparison to his own generation he was a fairly righteous man, but the moment he saw the King in splendor and beauty is also the moment the veil over his own soul was lifted. He was able to clearly see the depths of darkness and sin in his own soul for the first time, hence he cried out, "Woe is me!"

What Isaiah saw is also the same condition in which all of mankind currently resides. Before the eyes of the Lord, no one does well, none seek him. Like sheep, we have all gone astray in the pursuits of our evil hearts (Jeremiah 17:9). As a result, we are enemies of the throne, a virus that is no better than the demons of hell. As extreme as that comparison may sound, those who reject the gospel will suffer the same fate as Lucifer and his fallen angels (Matthew 25:41). Throughout the Bible we are described as mere objects of dust, seeds, and wheat that are of little value and usage. In our current condition, we have no value or beauty that the Lord should look upon us.

The Heart of the Son

Though man has fallen so short of the glory of God and stands in utter darkness, the Son in eternity past said to the Father:

Father, those whom you have given me, I will redeem them. Though they have sinned and rebelled against us, I will bring them back into your presence. I will empty myself and take on the form of a servant and humble myself to take on the form of man. Behold, I delight to do your will, and with the body which you have prepared for me, I will carry out your plan. I will lay down My life for theirs; out of the anguish of my soul, they shall be made righteous before your eyes. I will tell of your name to my brothers so that they may sing praises to your holy name. That plan though comes with great cost, for to save them means to be forsaken by you Father—something I have never known or experienced. To satisfy your wrath, I will pour out my soul to death, so that the love with which you have loved me may be in them, and I in them.

The Humility of the Son

Though man does not deserve life or a second chance, the Son, in an incredible act of love, humbled himself to the point where he would have to sacrifice everything—just to be able to breathe life into our souls once again. He who dwells in perfection and is forever caught in the eternal love that flows between the Father and Spirit is the very one Job caught a glimpse of: "I had heard of you by the hearing of the ear, but now my eyes see you; therefore I despise myself, and repent in dust and ashes" (Job 42:5, 6). He is also the very one who would temporarily restrict his own divinity and humble himself lower then Job was ever capable of doing (Philippians 2:6-9). To become lesser than Job is to become lower than "dust and ashes"—the very attitude which Job expressed upon himself after seeing a glimpse of God's excellency.

Dust and ashes is what we are. From the dust we came, and to the dust we shall return. To think that the Son would subject himself to our hands is almost unthinkable, yet he has a pattern of doing the unthinkable. "But I am a worm and not a man, scorned by mankind and despised by the people" (Psalm 22:6). These words, which were penned by David's hand, are also the very words of Christ in this beautiful prophetic chapter. He may have been in the form of man, but he was still the Lord of glory, shining in blazing beauty! "And he was transfigured before them, and his face shone like the sun, and his clothes became white as light" (Matthew 17:2). Like a solar eclipse, the beauty and light of the sun may be obscured temporarily; nevertheless, it remains the sun shining in full strength. So it is also with the Son. He may have taken upon the nature of man, but he never lost his divine essence. The external manifestation of his glory was only temporarily obscured with his ministry on earth.

Sadly, no one was able to truly see or comprehend who he really was outside the help of the Father. When people saw this Man claiming to be the Son of God, the Messiah, many thought he was speaking blasphemy. In their eyes "he had no form or majesty that we should look at him, and no beauty that we should desire him" (Isaiah 53:2). And so mankind rejected the giver of life and preferred darkness rather than light.

The Love of the Son

However, all such opposition would not deter the Son of God but would only become fuel for his glory—the very same glory of the Father that was the heartbeat of the Son's life and ministry. Namely, the divine love of God that knows no bounds and cannot be broken is also the same love the Son would place upon humanity. To do so would imply his love would bear any trial that was set before him, believe that mankind could be redeemed and brought back into the presence of the Father, hope all things and becomes a living conviction, endure right to the very end and never stop loving. That kind of love would drive the Son to bear the trials of sorrow and griefs of being rejected by men. "He was despised and rejected by men; a man of sorrows, and acquainted with grief" (Isaiah 53:3). Love would enable the Son to bear the weight of sin upon his own shoulders. He would take away all of our sorrows and griefs that come from this world of sin; but more importantly, he would endure the very wrath of God that was reserved for us:

> Surely he has borne our griefs and carried our sorrows; yet we esteemed him stricken, and smitten by God, and afflicted. But he was pierced for our transgressions; he was crushed for our iniquities; upon him was the chastisement that brought us peace, and with his wounds we are healed. All we like sheep have gone astray; we have turned everyone to his own way; and the LORD has laid on him the iniquity of us all. (Isaiah 53:4-6)

As he was being nailed to the cross, the watching world thought he was being executed for treason, rebellion, and blasphemy. In reality, every time those nails were struck, he was bearing our griefs and our sorrows upon his own shoulders. The very realties and horrors of sin, every sorrow, and every pain that was ever caused by sin was placed upon him (v. 4). He took it all, for upon him was the chastisement that belonged to us. A chastisement that one could only begin to imagine would cause the Son to cry out to up on high: "Father, if you are willing, remove this cup from me. Nevertheless, not my will, but yours, be done" (Luke 22:42).

That chastisement would cause him to sweat drops of blood. "And being in agony he prayed more earnestly; and his sweat become like great drops of blood falling down to the ground" (v. 44). That chastisement equaled the totality of every sin ever committed: "...and the LORD has laid on him the iniquity of us all" (Isaiah 53:6).

We, as the human race, have lived in iniquity and transgressed against the Lord our entire life; our entire society is based and built upon the foundation of iniquity. When light came into the world, we preferred darkness rather than the light of life, for we like sheep have gone astray, everyone to his own way. In our hearts we committed the same act of treason as Satan as we have established our own throne, our own standard, and our own righteousness based on darkness. Yet Christ's chastisement would breathe hope into the souls of mankind; his chastisement would cause the morning star to shine once again within our hearts (cf. 2 Peter 1:19). For by the love of the Son and the wounds of the Son, are we healed (Isaiah 53:5).

Dear Heavenly Father, thank you for your plan before the foundation of the world. Thank you for your one and only begotten Son. Without your love, we would be lost in darkness, yet you would not have it so. Jesus, thank you for being mindful of us, for being willing to give up everything so that we could come home and be in your presence. By your wounds, we are healed to know you and to love you unto all eternity. Amen.

CHAPTER 3

Risen Unto Eternity

Moments of Darkness

As Jesus was enduring the crucifixion, some of his last moments upon this earth were also some of the darkest times upon the earth: "there was darkness over the whole land until the ninth hour" (Luke 23:44). In those moments he was forsaken by his own Father. "My God, my God, why have you forsaken me?" (Matthew 27:46). It would have appeared as if the forces of darkness prevailed, and the light was quenched. Regardless, even in the darkest moments—the likes of which this world has never seen—the rays of hope were still shining through the clouds. In his last moments, in his last words as he said "It if finished," he was proclaiming words of victory and life. It is only in the darkest moments of life that light and hope begin to shine from on high. So it was with the Son; only in his darkest hour did the light begin to break through and turn the tides against the forces of evil.

The Declaration of the Son

As he spoke his final words, he, in effect, was committing his Spirit into the hands of his Father and passed from this life to the next (Luke 23:46). Although he died, it was through death that he destroyed the power of death and the one who wielded it (Hebrews 2:15). The Lord of glory was risen back to life because it was impossible that he should be held by death (Acts 3:24). The righteous for the unrighteous, though he was put to death in the flesh, he was made alive in the Spirit with a primary emphasis of bringing man back into the presence of his Father (1 Peter 3:18). The desire and heart of the Son was to carry out his Father's will, which was to bring mankind home to eternal glory.

The moment the Son was resurrected back to life by the glory of the Father is also the moment he received his inheritance and was declared to be the Son of God in power and glory (Romans 1:4). In essence, his resurrection could be perceived not only as a declaration, but also as his coronation unto the throne of glory. The Son is the radiance of the glory of his Father and of the same divine essence; he alone upholds the universe by the word of his power because he endured that which no one else could, namely, the wrath of God. In doing so, he made purification for sin and was given the right to take his place upon the throne of the Majesty On High or rather his Father's throne (Hebrews 1:3).

The Love of the Trinity in the Soul of Man

When the Son died and was raised back to life, he was not alone; for he took a host of captives with him:

> We were buried therefore with him by baptism
> into death, in order that, just as Christ was raised

> from the dead by the glory of the Father, we too
> might walk in newness of life. (Romans 6:4)

As the Son died, so too did we die with him. It is not a figure of speech or metaphor but a statement of fact as he emphasizes the point with the word "therefore." It's a fact that should be written into our subconscious for we died with him by *baptism* or "immersion," meaning that in a spiritual way, we were immersed into his death and our old self has passed from existence. It may not have been a literal physical death of which we were consciously part of; nevertheless, it still happened in ways we cannot fully conceive or understand. In the same way we were buried in his death, we were also raised from the dead by the glory of the Father and now walk in the newness of life. And this newness of life into which we have now entered is the love of God shed abroad in our hearts. "God's love has been poured into our hearts through the Holy Spirit who has been given to us" (Romans 5:5).

Another way of saying it is the very life of the Trinity now resides within our very souls and because "the Holy Spirit has been given to us," the entire Trinity has now made their home within the inner depths of our hearts (John 14:17-23). The forever blessed Trinity that resides in eternity—a world that is an ocean of divine love and endless joy—has now made their home of infinite perfection inside of every believer. Such a thought cannot fully be conceived or comprehended while in this world, but even a glimpse of this glory has the power to move the heart of any child of God. For to have the triune God residing within our souls also means that divine love is now the driving principle guiding and regulating our once lost hearts. Such a statement also implies that the very perfections or attributes that constitute who God is has now been infused into our souls.

Divine Love, the Sum and Totality of God's Nature

As the light from the sun may shine on a flawless diamond and emanate different reflections of light from the sun revealing the beauties of the diamond, the source itself remains the same. The different reflections of light are still the same beams shining from the sun, and the beauties themselves are simply different aspects of the same diamond. So it is with every attribute or exercise of grace with God. Every attribute or perfection of the divine excellency has divine love as being the core of its firm foundation.

As patience, kindness, joy, peace, and faithfulness are all fruits of the Spirit, they are also particular attributes of God's nature. Therefore, they are also different expressions of divine love. "Love is patient and kind" refers to God's attributes of patience and kindness. "Believes all things, hopes all things" can be referring to faith and hope (1 Corinthians 13:4-7). This in turn means that the very attributes or reflections of God's character all stem and flow forth from one thing, *divine love.* This nature is evidenced in many places, but in particular in the fruits of the Spirit, which are labeled as *fruit* not *fruits* in Scripture (Galatians 5:22). So for "love" to be listed as the first fruit means that all of the others flow forth from love being the core, especially in light of the particular word choice immediately prior to the fruit being listed.

Another example where this can be more clearly seen is Romans 13:8 and 13:10. In this passage the law is being defined and summed up in its entirety by Paul as *love* "for the one who loves another has fulfilled the law" (v. 8), and "love is the fulfilling of the law" (v. 10). This is most uniquely important because every law reflects some attribute of God's nature in some way, yet the entirety of it is summed up simply in *love.*

If all of God's attributes can be summed up in *love*, it is because all of them flow forth from love. So to highlight particular attributes like justice or peace is also to say they originate from love yet are different expressions or reflections of love itself. All of God's attributes are connected and overlap each other in some way; there is no such thing as God's attributes being independent of one another or their being at odds with one another. Quite simply, they are all connected as one and operate as one, yet in unique ways with love being the core and chief brightness of them all.

God is one (Deuteronomy 6:4), so it should be of no surprise that as the Trinity acts as *one* in everything that they do, so also does God's nature function as *one*. The greatest example is the Cross of Christ, as every attribute of God was on display at the Cross in utter unique fashion and emanated in several different ways. For instance, the wrath of God was poured out onto the Son, so that mercy, love, and grace could be poured out onto us.

As streams of water may flow down different paths along the earth and from different angles, each stream can emanate various expressions of itself; nevertheless, it's still the same water flowing from the same fountain. The streams are the various exercises of grace all flowing forth from the same fountain, namely the divine love of the triune God. As a result, divine love can be said to be the summation and totality of God's glorious attributes.

Excellency Infused into the Soul of Man

Allow me to bring everything together up to this point. To have the love of God poured into our hearts by the Holy Spirit (Romans 5:5) also means we have been given the Spirit as an inheritance or rather as a down payment—a gift (Ephesians 1:13, 14). The Spirit or rather the Trinity now resides within us, the very perfections of God's excellency now flow as rivers of life within our very hearts. "Out of his heart will flow rivers of living water." (John 7:38). In other words, to have God's love poured into our hearts also means every exercise of grace or God's attributes have now become the very fabric of our character because divine love is the totality or sum of all grace.

Risen for Glory

The very glory that brought us life is now the very heartbeat of our lives for we have died to the world and the world to us. The things of this world are passing and fleeting, but that which is eternal is now the objective of our lives. We were once dead in our trespasses, but out of the ashes we have risen into new life given to us by the glory of the Father. Our souls have been ignited as a holy flame from on High and have now entered into a life of glory. Upon this grace which we stand, we no longer live for ourselves; rather, we live for him who died for us.

Life with the Son

The moment we were raised with Christ is also the moment we became one spirit with him (1 Corinthians 6:17). To die with the Son and to be raised with the Son means our lives and identities are now one with the Son in every way imaginable. The life the Son has within the Trinity has now become our life. As the Father has chosen his Son to be the express image of his glory (2 Corinthians 4:6), so the Son has chosen us to be the instruments of his glory (John 17:22). The infinite joy and delight of the Son has also been passed onto us (17:13), for we have also entered into an ocean of divine love that has always flowed between the Father and the Son with the Spirit from eternity past. The Father now looks upon us with the same love and affection he has for his Son (17:23). And the very love the Father has for the Son has now been passed onto us, so that we also may adore and delight ourselves in his perfections for all of eternity (17:26).

A Kingdom of Divine Love

It could be said that we have already entered into a realm of heaven on earth because we are one with the Son. In eternity we shall forever behold and delight ourselves in the glory of God. Heaven is the Lord's dwelling place (1 Kings 8:49), and from there the full radiance and brightness of his glory shines forth (Revelation 21:22-25). After all, heaven is a world without blight, sin, iniquity, darkness, or anything that could possibly obscure the Son of righteousness from shining forth his beauty and splendor. As the law itself is an expression of every attribute of God in some way and can be summed up as love (Romans 13:10), so heaven itself can be defined as a world of divine love blazing forth as bright as the noonday sun. Jonathan Edwards describes the reality of such a blessed world:

> There dwells God the Father, and so the Son, who are united in infinitely dear and incomprehensible mutual love. There dwells God the Father, who is the Father of mercies, and so the Father of love, who so loved the world that he gave his only begotten Son, that whosoever believeth in him should not perish, but have everlasting life [John 3:16]. There dwells Jesus Christ, the Lamb of God, the Prince of peace and love, who so loved the world that he shed his blood, and poured out his soul unto death for it.
>
> There dwells the Mediator, by whom all God's love is expressed to the saints, by whom the fruits of it have been purchased, and through whom they are communicated, and through whom love is imparted to the hearts of all the church. There Christ dwells in both his natures, his human and divine, sitting with the Father in⁸ the same throne.

There is the Holy Spirit, the spirit of divine love,
in whom the very essence of God, as it were, all
flows out or is breathed forth in love, and by whose
immediate influence all holy love is shed abroad
in the hearts of all the church [cf. Romans 5:5].
There in heaven this fountain of love, this eternal
three in one, is set open without any obstacle to
hinder access to it. There this glorious God is
manifested and shines forth in full glory, in beams
of love; there the fountain overflows in streams
and rivers of love and delight, enough for all to
drink at, and to swim in, yea, so as to overflow the
world as it were with a deluge of love. [1]

The Kingdom of Glory Is at Hand

The moment we became one with the Son and the love of God was shed abroad in our hearts is the moment we entered into a kingdom of glory. We imagine and long to enter into heaven one day, but, for the believer, that life has already started because the Spirit of Christ dwells inside of us. Heaven is a world of love, and that love or principle already resides within us. We live and breathe the glory of Christ. God the Father raised the Son from the dead and gave him glory so that our faith and hope are *in him* and not the world (1 Peter 1:21). The glory of the Son is the reason why we even have breath in this world; it's also the reason why we were originally created (Isaiah 43:7).

We are called to seek the kingdom of God and his righteousness above all else. "But seek first the kingdom of God and his righteousness, and all these things will be added to you" (Matthew 6:33). I believe the kingdom of God can be summed up as the following: "For the kingdom of God is not a matter of eating or drinking but of righteousness and peace and joy in the Holy

Spirit" (Romans 14:17). Righteousness, peace, and joy are some of the firm foundations of God's kingdom; they are also attributes of the divine nature.

For this reason, I believe the command to seek God's kingdom above all else can be narrowed down even further. "So, whether you eat or drink, do all to the glory of God" (1 Corinthians 10:31). To seek God's glory in everything that you do is also seeking God's kingdom above all else. In other words, because God's glory can be summed up as the beauty of his divine nature or the totality of whom God is, every circumstance in life is an opportunity to display an attribute of the divine nature, or rather God's glory. Because divine love is the firm foundation and the chief brightness of his glory, to seek and display the love of God is also to seek his kingdom and glory in any and every situation in life.

Inevitably one may raise the question, "That sounds beautiful and nice, but how does a person go about seeking God's glory or displaying his love in every situation in life?" Well I'm glad you asked because the answer is even simpler! Though that answer is still complex because of the world in which we live, nevertheless, the answer is still a simple one.

Fellowship with the Son

The answer is seek after the only begotten Son of God. For every duty that the Christian life requires, i.e., seeking God's kingdom, seeking his glory, loving your neighbor as yourself, and so forth, can all be further narrowed down by your love relationship with the Son. Because divine love is the totality or summation of all grace and fulfilling all the duties of the Christian life is dependent upon the exercises of grace, therefore all can be traced back to the Son himself. As love is the chief radiance of all of his glory, it is also the essence of his nature (1 John 4:16). Therefore, my friend, seeking after the Son and making your love relationship with him the first priority in your life will enable you to live the abundant Christian life. Ephesians alludes to this truth:

That according to the riches of his glory he may grant you to be strengthened with power through his Spirit in your inner being, so that Christ may dwell in your hearts through faith that you, being rooted and grounded in love, may have strength to comprehend with all the saints what is the breadth and length and height and depth, and to know the love of Christ that surpasses all knowledge, that you may be filled with all the fullness of God. (Ephesians 3:16-19)

For Christ to be at home within your heart, the inevitable conclusion is your communing and having fellowship regularly through the power of the Spirit (v. 16). If that be the case, then inevitably your soul ("that you, being rooted and grounded in love") is being ignited as a flame of divine love. With love being the firm foundation in your heart, everything else will begin to flow naturally. The longer you walk with the Son in your everyday life, the more you will begin to see and understand through the eyes of faith the depths of God's love (v.18). Having such wonderful knowledge from experiencing it firsthand will also bring with it the transforming power of his glorious grace, or rather to be "filled with all the fullness of God" (v.19), thus also fulfilling and completing every duty required of the life of a believer.

The more the saved person beholds the glory of God from the heart, the more he will be transformed into the same glory—from one degree of glory to another (2 Corinthians 3:18). In other words, to walk with God in everyday life through the means of grace that he provides, Christ will begin to dwell in your heart, thus inflaming your soul as a holy flame of love. As a result, your love relationship with God will soar to new heights like never before and, as earlier stated, love is the center from which all other grace flows forth. Your life will be transformed in every other way as a byproduct from the overflow of your love relationship with God.

To focus too much on one's sanctification, habitual sin, duties of life, or even the means of grace like Bible reading or listening to sermons can stunt the believer's growth. He may begin to lose sight of the reason for those blessings, for they were given as the God-ordained means to have fellowship and to walk with him. Over time, an attitude of humility may slowly turn into one of pride, and what was once a means of grace may become a means of self-righteousness.

For instance, even though we have been redeemed and walk in the newness of life, indwelling sin is still present and easily deceives us. We have the tendency to pursue those things in life, yet we do so in our own will power or according to the flesh. The remaining depths of darkness of sin still residing within us are overwhelming to say the least. The more a believer matures in the Christian life through the Spirit, the more he will become aware of the abundant darkness still lurking within. I believe Paul best illustrates this truth as he describes himself in Romans 7:14-25. At this point he was a very mature Christian nearing the end of his life. However, this topic will be addressed in further detail in a later chapter. At this particular juncture, we will keep our eyes fixed on the Son and remember that if we seek him and his glory first and foremost, everything else will fall into place.

Heaven in the Heart

For the Son to be living and reigning in the heart only comes when we invite and yield our hearts to him. An amazing paradox in the Bible is that even though our sovereign God will decree the happening of something, that pronouncement will never happen outside the will of an individual. For instance, even though some are chosen by God to believe in the Son, salvation happens in cohesion with that individual's will—not outside of it. However, that does not mean or imply that some were chosen because they would choose God. It means that human responsibility or the faculty of our wills is an element or component in the outworking of his sovereignty. The point is that for Christ to dwell in our hearts by faith, we must earnestly strive and seek after him daily. Then and only then will we fulfill every responsibility given to us by the Father or begin to experience a glimpse of the riches of heaven as exiles on the earth (cf. Hebrews 11:13-16).

When the Son is at home in the heart, there is "joy that is inexpressible and filled with glory" (1 Peter 1:8). It's the life of God in the soul of man; it's the soul of man entering into the realm of heaven even as a pilgrim on the earth. Heaven is a world of divine love like no other, so as Christ resides within the soul of man, our citizenship in heaven has already begun. "But our citizenship is in heaven..." (Philippians 3:20). And our citizenship to such a world gives us the rights and privileges of entering into the life of the Trinity and walking in fellowship in this life and in the eternal one to come. To walk in fellowship with the Son brings greater delight and joy than anything this world has to offer. That which is physical and temporal can never satisfy an immortal soul. While the happiness of this life is dependent upon circumstances, it only brings temporal peace that comes and goes like the wind.

The joy that comes from the life of the Trinity is incomprehensible and unbreakable for this joy is not dependent upon circumstances or the pleasures of life. Even if everything around you is falling apart and no joy can be found, there is always hope. Like Paul, we can find joy even in a world of troubles and sorrows. Though we may be sorrowful at times—"as sorrowful, yet always rejoicing" (2 Corinthians 6:10)—yet we are always rejoicing because our true life is forever intertwined into the blessed Trinity through the Son. Peace like a river floods its way into the heart of a believer. The soul begins to find abiding, satisfying peace; tranquility; and serenity the likes of which it has never known. Jonathan Edwards best describes the joys and fruits of such a life:

> *The other fruit of this love in heaven exercised*
> *in such circumstances is perfect tranquility and*
> *joy. Holy, humble and divine love is a principle of*
> *wonderful power to give ineffable quietness and*
> *tranquility to the soul. It banishes all disturbance,*
> *it sweetly composes and brings rest, it makes*
> *all things appear calm and sweet. In that soul*
> *where divine love reigns, and is in lively exercise,*
> *nothing can raise a storm.* [2]

Although Edwards is describing the reality and nature of heaven for the believer; nevertheless, his portrayal still applies, to a lesser degree, to pilgrims on the earth. His is a greater description of what Paul said in 2 Corinthians 6:10, "sorrowful, yet always rejoicing," for his soul was rooted and grounded in the divine. His focus was so upward that he still experienced supernatural quietness and tranquility in his inner being despite his outward conditions. We have been called to live this life also, for we have been given everything necessary for life and godliness in this present age. Outside of the Son, there is no lasting peace or joy. Still, we have been given the greatest gift of all—the only begotten Son of the Father and the endless pleasures that come with him. However, many obstacles would seek to stop or hinder our pursuit of the Son at all cost.

Pick Up Your Cross

Living for the Son and seeking God's kingdom through him is the greatest delight and joy one can experience while still in this world. Nonetheless, experiencing that joy comes at a great price. For to seek his kingdom and to have a foretaste of heaven in this life also means we must deny ourselves and pick up our cross. "If anyone would come after me, let him deny himself and take up his cross daily and follow me" (Luke 9:23). *To deny self* means "to forsake the pleasures and comforts of this world." You must become at odds with this world, which can mean the loss of popularity, friends, particular jobs, family, perhaps even your own spouse or children (cf. Matthew 10:34-39).

The believer must be willing to lose everything in this life in order to follow Christ. We have conditioned our souls to find rest and comfort within the temporal things of this life. However, eternity has been written into the fabrics of our hearts (Ecclesiastes 3:11). meaning our souls shall find no lasting rest or peace within the confines of this world. Jesus himself said it best: "Whoever finds his life will lose it, and whoever loses his life for my sake will find it" (Matthew 10:39).

If you do find your purpose or identity in this life, you will wake up one day and discover that was never your life, for you were created for a higher purpose. Moreover, if you deny yourself and walk the path the he once walked, namely the path to glory through suffering, then and only then will you begin to discover the real meaning and purpose of life. Your life is not your own for you have died and are now hidden with Christ in God. Indeed, you no longer live, but rather Christ who lives in you (Galatians 2:20).

The Love of the World

The advantages and blessings that come from seeking after the Son are innumerable, and there is no need to belabor the subject at this point except to note that seeking after the divine excellency through the Son is the greatest nobility and achievement to which one can aspire in this life or the eternal one to come. Any well-educated soul who has seen the loveliness of the divine perfections knows this, yet that person is also likely to be intimately aware of the constant struggle that comes from this pursuit. The heart of a believer may ebb and flow from the love of God to the love of the world. While this pursuit may be the greatest, it is also one of the most difficult in which to engage. The soul may be regenerated and brought back to life to God, but seeds of corruption still remain.

These corruptions have persuaded and trained our souls to seek life where there is none. The love of the world may bring temporal pleasure; at best, it merely entertains our spirits all the while producing and yielding no lasting benefits. At best, our affections and pursuit of God are often hindered while our interest in self-love grows all the more. Our sense and pleasure of the divine perfections begins to wane and, like a lost sheep, we forget what it is like to walk with God. Sadly, we begin to settle for lesser things.

The logical person who has seen and tasted both worlds will conclude that the pursuit and love of this world is worthless and vain. To be engulfed in the pursuit of worldly pleasures and interests will only leave the soul lost, depressed, and raging for something more. In the end, all of those pleasures will pass away and only produce sorrow and regret as that person leaves this world for the next.

However, for an individual to simply acknowledge this truth or resolve to seek higher things will not suffice. The condition and nature of our being is like that of a lost sheep—always straying to and fro from one thing to another. One moment we are filled with awe and love for God; the next we are more concerned about our favorite movie and actually convince ourselves watching it will bring equal, if not greater, enjoyment than the presence of God. Such a resolution to abstain or fall out of love with the world requires diligent practice of daily watchfulness of our thoughts and actions, as well as the prudent necessity of preaching the truth to our hearts every single day.

Worth It All

One moment the pursuit of the Son will be worth it all, and we, like the psalmist, can sing from our hearts: "Whom have I in heaven but you? And there is nothing on earth I desire besides you" (Psalm 73:25). The next moment we are like David, straying like a lost sheep and finding ourselves lost in a sea of darkness until our souls begin to cry out desperately to God for redemption (Psalm 119:176). It is truly amazing that we are capable of enjoying the riches and love that flows between the Father and Son. Then, in an instant, we quickly forget that we are his and what he went through to call us his own. Such a vacillating reveals the nature and condition of our lost souls. For without Christ, who is the Shepherd and Overseer of our souls, we would forever wonder in darkness seeking but never finding rest.

Just as bacteria and viruses are devastating and contrary to physical health, so it is with iniquity and vices to the human soul. We were created to be image bearers of God and to do good—not evil (Jeremiah 13:23). Yet we are conditioned by sin to seek and love vices which are completely contrary to the nature of God. It's like falling in love with poison; the soul is not designed for such things, leaving in its wake only grief, sorrow, bitterness, and unrest.

The former should be avoided at all costs, and seeking the world above the Son will only produce these effects. To truly know and understand the realities of the world in which we live would quickly drive any person into an ocean of sorrow, driving them to seek either escape or to learn amnesia in a matter of seconds. Oftentimes the former is the hope they lean on, building up layers of defense through self-righteousness, false religion, busyness of life, and so forth.

The salvation of our souls is dependent upon our walk and how we value the Son. To say from the bottom of our hearts that he is worth it all will invariably mean we have seen and tasted

55

the virtues of his excellency or his divine nature. Virtues like humility yield greater delight and satisfaction to the heart than any vice ever could. Vices like bitterness, anger, envy, and idolatry only produce death. On the other hand, virtues leave the soul in a state of serenity—as if from walking with Christ in the garden of God, or watching a morning sunrise from the coastline. When virtues rule and reign in the heart, they bring the soul to a state of inner rest and peace. The results, however, are of far greater quality when of a spiritual nature, which is only produced *through the* Spirit of God by *seeking* the Son of God.

Because of who he is, what he has done for us, and for the sake of our loved ones, we should be more resolved than ever to count Christ as our most supreme treasure and joy. Christ is far more valuable than the finest treasures this world has to offer, not to mention the benefits far eclipse any pleasure or experience within this temporal life. Even to the simple-minded heaven is a world of far greater beauty and joy than this one. To have Christ dwelling richly in our hearts through faith is to experience heaven on earth. So if heaven is so great, shouldn't Christ be worth all of the trials and hardships of this world? Shouldn't Jesus be greater than any adrenaline rush, any relationship, or even marriage which is considered to be the grace of this life? Such tangibles are only a reflection of the worth and excellency of the Son. Because we have been raised unto eternity, let us be resolved to testify from our hearts that the Son is truly worth it all! Through any storm, insult, hardship, trial, calamity, or even death itself Christ is worth it all.

> *Dear Heavenly Father, thank you for raising us unto new life with and through your one and only begotten Son. We are unworthy of the newness of life which we have been given by your glorious grace. Help us to understand the worth of your Son and to seek him above all else. Grant us a spirit of wisdom and understanding to*

walk worthy of our new life. Let our eyes be fixed upon you through your Son and let us see and understand the world through your eyes. By your grace help keep our ever-wandering hearts from unbelief and let us experience your love and the realities of heaven in ways we can only imagine. Amen.

CHAPTER 4

The Battle Within

Though the Son himself has fought for us, lived for us, died for us, redeemed us to call us his own, breathed life into our souls, enabling us to breathe fresh air once again, a battle still rages within the very heart of a child of God. True, our old self has died and the dominion of sin has been brought to an end (Romans 6:6). However, the presence and power of indwelling sin is still very real, and unfortunately this battle within rages on every minute of our lives.

The moment a person chooses to no longer fight and be vigilant in this war is the moment he has lost and surrendered to the dominion of sin (6:12). However, before addressing the battle itself and how to mortify sin, we must understand the nature and power of indwelling sin. Every believer must know his enemy in order to defeat his enemy.

The Nature of Sin

Sin in the Bible is oftentimes personified as a force or an entity (7:17). An agent of chaos bent on nothing but the desolation and destruction of the world which God has created, sin is everything that is contrary to the nature and beauty of God. At its core, it is self-seeking and self-exalting—pride, which is the foundation from which every fruit it bears comes. Sin's very nature is the complete opposite of God's nature and does everything in its power to oppose it.

More specifically, if sin cannot cause the believer to carry out its fruits of evil (Galatians 5:19-21), it will do everything in its power to hinder his walk with Christ (5:17). That is why things that aren't inherently evil but are neutral, such as movies or relationships, will become sin's chosen tool of increasing the love of the world in a person's heart, which is why Scripture warns and reminds those who love God to love not the world nor the things in the world (1 John 2:15-17).

One of sin's most effective means of accomplishing its objectives is through deceiving the individual through sinful desire. Sinful desire does not originate from a believer; rather, it comes from indwelling sin (Romans 7:17). As a result, many will look upon themselves as the source of those thoughts or desires not fully realizing it is sin trying to work through them. The reality is we are always engaged in an internal battle, and we are commanded by Scripture to present our "members" which encompasses our mind, will, and emotions as instruments of righteousness (Romans 6:15-23).

It is important to understand and recognize the distinct difference between sinful desire which comes from sin and our new identities in Christ. The reality of sinful desire, which manifests itself through thoughts in our minds, is that it is the enemy is working vigorously to deceive us into thinking we are the source. As a result, the believer is unable by the power of Christ to take every thought captive into the obedience of Christ (2 Corinthians 10:5). In other words, we will be able to turn those sinful thoughts into godly thoughts, prayer, or even discard them entirely because we recognize that its originating from indwelling sin—not ourselves.

However, if you are caught up in yourself through shame, depression, self-justification, or playing any "woe-is-me card," you have fallen prey to the deceitfulness of sin. Nevertheless, there is a clear distinction between recognizing the source of sin and taking responsibility for your own actions. When Paul recognized the source of sin, he took responsibility for anything he did (Romans 7:23, 24). The lesson to be learned is that an enemy lurks within, and indwelling sin is always at work trying to cause us to sin. Therefore, it is important to know and understand the source of temptation, but at the same time to take responsibility for any action that we do commit.

The Deception of the Exodus Generation

Sin is notorious for enslaving an individual through deception and causing him to harden his own heart. Such was the case for the Exodus generation of Israelites from Egypt. The vast majority of them saw miracle upon miracle beginning with the ten plagues to the parting of the Red Sea. Nevertheless, most of them went astray in their hearts and never knew God; therefore, God struck them down and swore they would never enter his kingdom of rest (Hebrews 3:7-11).

Because they were Israelites, they believed that all was well and that they were saved. With absolute forbearance, God reached out to them with the gift of salvation (4:2); yet with stubbornness of heart and unbelief, they constantly tested him and refused to come to him (3:15-19). Though they heard the gospel message, the Bible says that through the deceitfulness of sin their hearts were hardened, and they fell away from the living God (3:12-13).

When considering that generation and the incredible blessings they received, they have to be the object of pity. After all, the miracle upon miracle that the Hebrew nation saw was seemingly of absolutely no help to their salvation. Though tragedy befell that generation, many lessons can be learned from them about the nature of sin and the human condition. For instance, some of them began too trust in the security of their souls simply from hearing the words of the covenant spoken to them by Moses. They would speak peace to themselves and bless their own hearts despite the fact they were walking in sin and worshipping false gods. In the end, this false security cost them their very lives for the Lord showed no mercy or forgiveness to those who intentionally walked away from him (Deuteronomy 29:18-20). Their hearts leading them astray was undoubtedly the work of indwelling sin.

Moreover, this truth can be carried over and applied to the modern-day church. Many have heard the gospel message, attend church regularly, and profess to know Christ, but the reality is that many of them will go before the throne of God and say, "Lord, Lord, did we not know you and do many things in your name?" (Matthew 7:21-22). He will sadly say to them, "I never knew you; depart from me, you workers of lawlessness" (7:23). This sad truth is the reality in which we live. Those who deal with unbelievers or people within the church who are caught in the deception of sin should not view them as wicked sinners; rather, they should be seen as an image bearer of God who needs to be rescued by the grace of God.

A Heart in Love in Darkness

Another essential and foundational truth that can be learned from that generation is that the Israelites used God as a means to pursue and love sin. For instance, time after time they would stray and wander from God; as a result, God would afflict and punish them for their unfaithfulness. They would inevitably turn from their wandering and sinful pursuits to seek after God, but only when his anger was turned upon them:

> When he killed them, they sought him; they repented and sought God earnestly. They remembered that God was their rock, the Most High God their redeemer. But they flattered him with their mouths; they lied to him with their tongues. Their heart was not steadfast toward him; they were not faithful to his covenant. (Psalm 78:34-37)

The very fact that they "…repented and sought God earnestly" (v. 34), yet "their heart was not steadfast toward him" (v. 37) reveals the nature and motivation behind their hearts. They repented and sought God not because they truly loved him or were grieved in their hearts that they had sinned against him; rather, they sought him earnestly because they loved their sin and saw God as a means to ending the disturbance in their walk of darkness.

A truly repentant heart sees sin for what it really is and is grieved deeply within yet not for his own sake, but for God's sake and his holy name. They, like David, realize that against God and God only have they sinned against (Psalm 51:4). The desire of their heart is to turn away from sin and that by any means necessary be cleansed so that they may be whiter than snow (51:7). The cry and longing of their heart is to have a pure heart so they can be restored to fellowship with God (51:10-12).

However, the same could not be said of the Exodus generation. They only "sought him" because he "killed them"; they were not truly repentant in their hearts. Through sin, their hearts had fallen in love with darkness and the corruption of the world. Thus they "flattered him with their mouths" and "lied to him with their tongues." A heart that is bent on sin only sees God as a means to appease their conscious or to end the consequences of their sin.

Hence, "their heart was not steadfast toward him" (v. 37), thus confirming and sealing the truth that they only saw God as a means to an end, namely, their love and pursuit of sin. A person may hate the consequences of sin because it interferes with self-love but, at the core, he would rather die than to part ways with his love of sin.

Applied to the Life of a Believer

In turn, this truth can be applied to a believer as well, for we may have a gracious heart alive unto God, but we are not exempt from the mistakes or condition of the Exodus generation. We may have passed from the domain of darkness into the kingdom of the Father's beloved Son, but within us still lies pockets of darkness in the members of our bodies. In other words, we may have a new heart and a new spirit (Ezekiel 36:26), but various sinful attitudes, thoughts, habits, and lifestyles are still present in our daily lives. Believers are as prone to using God and the people around them as a means to pursing sin (1 Peter 2:11).

Any believer can be engaged in habitual sin and caught in a never-ending cycle of sinning, repenting, and repeating. They are continually caught in this cycle because the roots of sin may run deep which may have been carried over from their former life or through negligence of mortifying sin. Consequently, sin may have a foothold over the believer's soul, corrupting the desires of their heart and thus causing them to fall in love with sin.

If that is indeed the case, then their repentance before God is false; they are not actually repenting or sorrowful toward God for their sin. They are grieved because of the consequences of their sin from a convicting conscience, loss of joy and serenity of their soul. They feel empty and void inside, but the moment the conscience brings its assault to an end by the mercies of God, they turn around and commit the same sin again. Moreover, the purpose for their pursuit of God through prayer, reading the Word, or any other means of grace has been revealed; they weren't seeking God to change and turn away from that particular sin, but rather they merely pursued him as a means to end the effects of sin.

These believers may hate the effects of sin, but their love for sin has not diminished in the slightest. This is and can be the state of any born-again believer. However, for the most part, this doesn't take place at a conscious level but rather at the subconscious. Through repeated actions over a long period of time, certain habits or thoughts are ingrained into our internal belief system. Most of our actions throughout the day are a result of subconscious convictions. Therefore, the process of healing and repentance can be a long, drawn-out battle for many believers.

So arises the question: what is the believer supposed to do in light of such an overwhelming opponent? The very deceitfulness of sin alone is enough to thwart the efforts of any Christian, for we are more familiar with a life of sin than we are of righteousness— not to mention the relentless onslaught of sin in the life of the believer. Sin, which is always at work, never stops, never relents; it's always attacking from the moment we wake up to the moment we sleep at night. John Owen explains:

> *Sin does not only abide in us, but is still acting, still laboring to bring forth the deeds of the flesh. When sin lets us alone we may let sin alone; but as sin is never less quiet than when it seems to be most quiet, and its waters are for the most part deep when they are still, so ought our contrivances against it to be vigorous at all times and in all conditions, even where there is least suspicion.* [3]

A Call to Fight

Only one option remains for the child of God in light of such an enemy, and that is the pursuit of something greater.

> For if you live according to the flesh you will
> die, but if by the Spirit you put to death the deeds
> of the body, you will live. (Romans 8:13)

This verse is a simple, yet very powerful, command and statement. If you fight, you will live; if you don't, you will die. The command is to mortify the flesh by the Spirit, for outside of the grace of God, our vain efforts alone will only bring us further into darkness. However, how does the believer go about using the Spirit as a means for the destruction of the flesh?

Freedom Through the Son

The next verse provides a more clearer indication of how we do that: "For all who are led by the Spirit of God are sons of God" (Romans 8:14). In other words, to be led by the Spirit means you are pursuing the Son of God with all of your heart and all of your might; for the main purpose and ministry of the Spirit to believers is the glorification of the Son (John 16:13, 14). Therein is the answer to all of the riddles thus far; the hope and deliverance from the nature of sin is only through the *Son* by seeking the *Son* (1 Peter 1:8, 9).

The same truths addressed in the previous chapters that enable believers to fulfill every duty required of the Christian life, i.e., battle the love of the world and enjoy a foretaste of heaven in the heart, are also the same truths that help us in the battle of indwelling sin. This is all accomplished by keeping our eyes fixed on the Son through the Spirit; the pursuit of seeing and beholding his glory becomes the primary prerogative in our lives. The glory of Christ is the very reason by which we were called into salvation and is also the means of how we escape the corruption of this world through sinful desire:

> His divine power has granted to us all things that pertain to life and godliness, through the knowledge of him who called us by his own glory and excellence, by which he has granted to us his precious and very great promises, so that through them you may become partakers of the divine nature, having escaped from the corruption that is in the world because of sinful desire. (2 Peter 1:3, 4)

Everything that is necessary for the pilgrimage of this life—whether it be the proper internal attitudes of the heart "pertain to life" or the external disposition of those virtues "and godliness"—is obtained through our intimate knowledge of the Son "...through the knowledge of him" (v. 3). The intimate knowledge of the Son is the essence and key to battling indwelling sin and escaping "the corruption that is in the world because of sinful desire" (v. 4). Essentially, intimate knowledge of the Son is the key to everything in the Christian life, for we were saved by his glory to become partakers of his glory, or "partakers of the divine nature."

These verses are filled with amazing theological truths that are essential to understanding deep truths of God and practicality of life. I find them quite fascinating because they are all connected like a circular truth; one is the essence and foundation of one truth while another is intricately connected to another.

For instance, the "knowledge of him" is the knowledge of Christ's character or attributes; it also has a very similar meaning of "glory and excellence" (v. 3), which was mentioned in a previous chapter and means the beauty and external emanation of God's divine nature. In other words, we were saved because of who God is, "who called us by his own glory and excellence" so that we would reflect his glory, i.e., "...become partakers of the divine nature" which is accomplished only through knowing and understanding who the Son is: "through the knowledge of him."

All of these truths are dependent and connected to God's glory being the source, the means, and ultimately the end purpose (Romans 11:36). These truths are also the means by which we engage and battle indwelling sin. The most effective means of escaping the realities of indwelling sin is to pursue the complete opposite—the divine nature through the promises of God (2 Peter 1:3, 4).

As already stated, it is through the knowledge of the Son or rather understanding the virtues and character of God that brings everything together. Therefore, taking a deeper look at particular attributes like divine love, humility, and holiness will be of eternal value. Though some of these truths were already addressed, they are of an eternal nature that can never be fully explained or comprehended while in this life. In many cases, the truths and realities of the Bible are constantly repeated from book to book; it's like looking at one side of a coin then transitioning to the next, indeed two different sides yet still the same coin.

Divine Love

Divine love is the crescent star and crown jewel of all of God's attributes. None shines brighter or emanates his eternal beauty with such radiance. Divine love is the source and life stream from which all other attributes flow forth and is the life stream of the human soul. It is the very thing that was breathed into our hearts at the moment of conversion by the Holy Spirit. It is that which raised us from death unto newness of life. If eternal love can quicken us to life, then most certainly, it can loosen the bondage of indwelling sin.

The Supremacy of Divine Love

> If I speak in the tongues of men and of angels, but have not love, I am a noisy gong or a clanging cymbal. And if I have prophetic powers, and understand all mysteries and all knowledge, and if I have all faith, so as to remove mountains, but have not love, I am nothing. If I give away all that I have, and if I deliver up my body to be burned, but have not love, I gain nothing. (1 Corinthians 13:1-3)

A person may be blessed with all of the greatest gifts and external abilities in the world, but if he does not possess love, he is simply nothing. Everything in which we engage in life is ultimately a means to an end—whether delivering a speech in front of thousands, cleaning dishes, having a distinguished career, or saving the world from impending doom. There is always a driving reason and end goal in mind when any person pursues these means. They often say that the ends justifies the means; however, in light of Scripture, if divine love is not the driving principle behind the means or the end goal, than ultimately that pursuit is worthless and profits nothing.

The value and supremacy of divine love is Paul's primary focus in the first three verses of I Corinthians 13. Especially note that all three verses repeat the phrase "...but have not love," which illustrates the end result—"I am nothing" or "I gain nothing." The value and worth of something is dependent upon divine love's being the driving principle behind it and resulting in the exaltation and emanation of divine love. If, in faithfulness to God, a believer is taking out the trash or pouring drinks for others and love is the driving force, than those efforts have eternal value and worth that will go on to all eternity. Compare that believer's driving force to the person who may have just saved the world or devoted his entire life to serving and helping others with no dependence upon God; those efforts will pass away with the wind and will hold no value because divine love was not the driving force or end goal.

External gifts and abilities hold no value or worth in and of themselves. They only hold value if they are used as a means to seek and emanate God's eternal love. God's love is life itself; therefore, it holds eternal value. To seek the means of everyday life as a means or way to emanate divine love is to use everyday life as a way to let life shine forth for all to see. In other words, to let eternal love be the understanding and motivation for one's business, helping one's family, and the like, is the equivalent of saying the means of everyday life becomes the tools or vessels by which life itself is exhibited or emanated for all to view.

In doing so, is to live life in a manner that is worthy of the Gospel (Philippians 1:27), which is also the greatest act of love one can possibly do. For to do so, is to guide others to rivers of living water (John 7:38), it's to give them the very life of their souls. Of which cannot and will never be found in this physical world, but only in the Gospel of Christ. It's its reason why Christ performed miracles and healed people throughout the Gospels, to show that coming to him will result in the healing and rest of their souls. Physical blessings will only go so far, but it's the spiritual blessings that will last unto eternity. For many were healed of their diseases and infirmities in Christ's day, but to what avail? They would become sick a month later or even die within a couple years, and yet the disease of their heart was not healed (Jeremiah 17:9). Grace and divine love upon the soul is the greatest blessing and healing one will ever find. Yet we as believers are chosen to guide those who do not know Christ to the ocean shores of the Gospel through our lives.

Knowing that the simple duties and responsibilities of everyday life are the means by which God has chosen to let eternal life shine forth will change anyone's perspective on even the most mundane activities. Without a proper understanding of the supremacy of divine love or a driving zeal to use everything within one's capacity to seek and exhibit that love, then all of an individual's efforts and achievements within this life will simply fade away with the passing winds of time. However, anything that is done in faithfulness to God for his name's sake, for love's sake, or the display of his love will carry on to all eternity.

The Ways and Perfections of Divine Love

> Love is patient and kind; love does not envy or boast; it is not arrogant or rude. It does not insist on its own way; it is not irritable or resentful; it does not rejoice at wrongdoing, but rejoices with the truth. Love bears all things, believes all things, hopes all things, endures all things. Love never ends. (1 Corinthians 13:4-8)

The ways of love should also be considered the ways of life. Without these ways or understandings, there would be no life inside the human soul. The believer should strive to understand the ways of life and emulate them in everyday life, so that all may see and have life for themselves inside the gospel of Christ.

The perfections of divine love begins with "love is patient and kind…." Patience is the stance and condition of the heart in light of any insult, trial, persecution, or hardship received from another. Kindness is the effectual response of the soul to any and every person despite his conduct. However, being kind does not exclude being firm or stern with others in the right circumstances; indeed, for some, this is an act of kindness.

Patience and kindness are merely different forms and expressions of love, which allows divine love to reign supremely unhindered within the soul as supernatural peace and joy reign therein. The state of the soul is abounding in heavenly bliss as those virtues overflow into the hearts and lives of others. Patience absorbs all external opposition, and kindness washes away the corruption of darkness. Sometimes the effects can be seen immediately while others require the element of time.

Understanding what love is makes it easy to distinguish and understand what love is not. Verses 4-7 contain 15 qualities of love, and each of these qualities are listed as verbs requiring action. The first two—"patient" and "kind"—are positive; the next eight are negative, and the last five are positive. The sum of the eight could be centered on "love does not insist on having its own way" (v. 5); genuine divine love seeks the ways of life or God's ways, which is the unconditional well-being of a person's soul or simply the best interest of everything in general. However, the effects of the person who insists upon having his own way will always be that of envying, boasting, arrogance, rudeness, irritability, resentment, and rejoicing at wrongdoing (1 Corinthians 13:4-7).

The last five positive qualities are like melodious tunes to the human heart. For love only rejoices with the truth (v. 6)— never at the theme of sin or iniquity and never at the expense or degradation of another. Love will only rejoice if life is being infused into the heart of another human being and never at the downgrading or dehumanizing of another. True love will bear with the faults of others and never gossip about them for the sheer delight of entertainment. The word *bear* (v. 7) has the meaning of "covering with silence." Love will genuinely and delightfully bear with the failings and faults of others for their sake. Divine love will not expose or be eager to shame others unless forced to by biblical standards like Matthew 18.

Love will "believe" the very best of someone and never willingly give in to dark suspicion or think negatively based upon appearances alone. It's to think and desire the very best of someone until reason alone forces a different conclusion; and even then, the godly do so with reluctance for they do not desire such things. After all, even God does not desire the death of the wicked nor rejoices in it (Ezekiel 18:32).

Indeed, times arise when circumstances may no longer allow a person to truly and honestly believe the very best. If that becomes the case, then one can also "hope" all things because their faith and foundation is not in themselves or the circumstances of life. On the contrary, their hope is in a sovereign God who works all things according to the counsel of his own will. In the end, love will bear any trial or circumstance thrown its way and will "endure" it right to the very end. Godly love conquers by perseverance and endurance.

Through it all, the things of this life will pass away, circumstances are temporal, and the pleasures of this life are never permanent. Divine love is one of the greatest virtues of God, and while everything within space and time will ultimately pass away, love will go on to all eternity. Love never ends (1 Corinthians 13:8).

Humility

Humility is the greatest achievement and nobility to which the human soul can aspire or attain. It's the ability of the human soul to look up on high and see God for who he really is and in light of that ability, to see his own true condition. In essence, it could be said that *humility is the recognition of oneself in light of who God is.* It's to no longer walk this earth in the blindness and corruption of sin, but rather to see the reality in which we live through the eyes of God. Those who are humble will reign with Christ on his throne, and they are stronger than the proud. For what takes greater strength? To restrain your own spirit in the midst of difficulty for the sake of others or to act out in anger for the sake of pride?

Humility is the greatest achievement and nobility of the human soul because it takes greater strength to live and walk in light of who we really are before God, than it is to live life under the delusion that we are something and that the world revolves around us. Greater is he who denies himself, acknowledges he has died, and his life is hidden with Christ in God (Colossians 3:3), than the one who lives under a false identity stemming from a diseased soul.

No greater example of humility exists than the second member of the Trinity, who regarded himself as nothing—though he is everything:

> Who, though he was in the form of God, did not count equality with God a thing to be grasped, but emptied himself, by taking the form of a servant, being found in human form, he humbled himself by becoming obedient to the point of death, even death on a cross. (Philippians 2:6-8)

These verses have great theological importance, but their original context is of a more practical implication. They are referred to as the ladder of infinite condescension—the steps the Son had to take in order to descend down to man. Each step is of great significance; with each step he gives up something dear to his heart.

Christ is one with the Father; therefore, they are equal in every way and are of the same divine essence (John 10:30; Hebrews 1:3). Though he was in the form of God, he was willing to give up his throne and submit himself to the will of the Father. He was willing to give up his rights of deity and chose not to live by those realities (v. 6). The Son went a step further by restricting the usage of his own divinity by not using his own power except in accordance with the Father's will. The next step required him to take on the form of a servant, but not simply any servant. He could have taken on the form of an angel or even pre-fallen man, but he took on the form of post-fallen man which was stepping to the lowest level he could go (v. 7).

Jesus chose to be defined by weakness, temptation, grief, sorrow—conditions of which he knew, but had never previously experienced (Hebrews 5:8, 9). Even his reputation was of no importance to him; through his own word and various miracles, he confirmed to the watching world that he was God in human form. Despite the fact that he was God, he was content with suffering false accusations and blasphemous statements that slandered his reputation. Moreover, by the will of God, Jesus was content with enduring a traitor's death—even death on a cross (v. 8).

The humble are those who are exalted before the throne of God—as Jesus himself was exalted by the Father for what he suffered and accomplished so that at the name of Jesus every knee should bow and every tongue confess that Jesus Christ is Lord, unto the glory of the Father (Philippians 2:9-11). Humility is a believer's recognition of himself in light of who God is, but it is also the means by which the child of God walks the path of glory through suffering. We are commanded to do nothing out of selfish ambition or conceit; to the contrary, we, in humility, are to count others more significant than ourselves. Possessing and displaying humility is only possible because of being one with Christ. Since we can also have the mind of Christ, humility is our firm duty and responsibility (Philippians 2:3-5). If the Son who is God himself could walk humbly before God the Father; then we who rightly deserve the wrath of God can also emulate the same walk.

Holiness

Holiness, which is very closely linked to humility and the pursuit thereof, has already been addressed, but primarily from God's view regarding his nature. One of the various aspects and definitions of holiness is "purity," which is essential to the walk of any believer. Purity is the recognition and pursuit of the higher qualities of God's virtues and the *abstinence* of sinful defilements or things of lesser value. The person who has tasted and seen that the Lord is good knows that nothing else can satisfy his soul for the virtues of God are the very life springs of the human soul. Understanding the divine love of God or delighting in expressions of humility toward others is to have the Spirit of life breathe grace into your heart.

Therein lays a transcending joy and a surpassing peace of the soul that only comes from God's virtues. To experience these godly virtues is to fall more in love with God and his glorious nature. As a result, the heart becomes more diligent and vigorous in its battle against anything that is of a contrary nature; more specifically, indwelling sin and even the neutral things of the world that can draw the believer's affections away from God. The more the life of God becomes infused into the soul, the more the child of God is willing to part ways with sin and the love of the world. The call to be holy becomes the very life of a child of God, for the soul knows that nothing but the Spirit himself can cause rivers of living water to flow from within.

Promises of Glory

The knowledge of God's virtues is the foundation for finding everything necessary for life and godliness, though only through the promises of glory do they become a reality in our lives (2 Peter 1:3, 4). In other words, becoming a partaker of the divine nature or pursuing Christlikeness is to be establishing the kingdom of heaven from within. In the pursuit of heaven in the heart, the child of God not only enjoys heaven on earth, but a byproduct is obtaining the salvation of his soul from indwelling sin. The promises of glory through Christ make these truths become practical reality in the lives of any believer. Many great biblical promises are given to us, but one in particular should breathe hope into the heart of any child of God:

> And we know that for those who love God all
> things work together for good, for those who are
> called according to his purpose. (Romans 8:28)

To truly understand and appreciate the depths of grace and love that encompasses this verse, some further background regarding the nature of "…all things work together…" is vital. For instance, the very structure and nature of this verse implies that God takes something that isn't good and overrides the end result according to his sovereign will. That which is contrary to good are the trials, tribulations, and calamities of life, which are the result of sin. God subjected the creation to futility as an act of judgment against original sin (Genesis 3:17-19; Romans 8:20).

As a result, the world now lies under the curse of sin and the external effects thereof. However, a distinct difference exists between the experience of the godly and the ungodly in these events. For example, though the believer may experience the same calamities as the ungodly, the very nature of those calamities and the internal results are entirely different. The internal composition or nature of afflictions for the unbeliever is the curse of sin, while the internal results of those afflictions on the soul are that of grief and sorrow. However, for the godly, the nature of afflictions are of grace and mercy with the internal results being the healing of the soul.

Thomas Watson elaborates:

> *Do not mistake me; I do not say that of their own nature the worst things are for good, for they are a fruit of the curse; but though they are naturally evil, yet the wise overruling hand of God disposing and sanctifying them, they are morally good. As the elements, though of contrary qualities, yet God has so tempered them, that they all work in a harmonious manner for the good of the universe. Or as in a watch, the wheels seem to move contrary one to another, but all carry on the motions of the watch: so things that seem to move cross to the godly, yet by the wonderful providence of God work for their good.*[4]

In other words, the afflictions that we dread and wish never to experience are actual gifts of mercy and grace stemming from God's eternal love. Through the cross those experiences of calamities need not be the same as an unbeliever, Christ himself took away the grief and sorrows that come from sin delivered to us by trials (Isaiah 53:4). An unbeliever experiences the full reality of such things; however, through prayer, the believer may experience outward sorrow, but inwardly he rejoices with unspeakable joy (2 Corinthians 6:10).

That joy, in fact, is the removal of the curse from afflictions replaced with the healing touch of God upon the soul. Afflictions and trials are the means by which God uses to flush out the corruption within our hearts and to heal the condition of our souls with his virtues (Hebrews 12:5-11). We learn to let go of the outward world to find everything we need in God himself, so that he and he alone is our all in all.

For this reason, everything is woven together for "good." The good can be implied of eternal blessing, but it is more specifically referring to a believer's heart being fashioned and conditioned to the nature of God. The soul becoming more of a partaker of the divine nature is of greater blessing and importance than any physical blessing we can receive. No external blessing can heal the corruption of sin that still haunts us, nor does it compare to the joy of heaven through God's virtues residing in our hearts. By experiencing such horrible afflictions and trials, we begin to see the reality of the world in which we live and begin to be thankful for receiving the Spirit of Christ. After all, in him and through him we find everything we need.

The natural nature and disposition of the soul is to seek anything but the fountain of life. So if God in his eternal love seeks to show us the folly of such things and the corruptions of our souls through trials, who are we to question and complain against him? Through such experiences we learn that we already have the greatest gift we could ever ask for, namely the Spirit of life himself (Luke 11:13). Upon this realization we begin to look inward, thus finding the greatest joy, tranquility, and serenity of the soul. Mankind, believers included, are constantly seeking life in circumstances when there is none—never realizing that having the virtues of God active in the soul is the greatest source of contentment, greater than any external circumstance could ever provide. No greater gift exists than the contentment of heaven in the heart through the virtues of God, despite the condition of the believer's circumstances.

Contentment—a Heavenly Spirit

Too truly understand the meaning of contentment, we must first understand its counterpart—discontentment, which ultimately is a vice springing from indwelling sin. The secret behind boredom; anxiety; stress; and a lack of joy, peace, and contentment is not seeking outward comfort, but the awareness that those vices stem from a sinful, prideful heart against God. What may seem small like being bored is a result of a failure of seeing the greater crime—the corruption of your own soul. The gift of heaven in the heart through the Spirit of life should result in joy and contentment—not a complaining grumbling attitude of Satan. However, the practical reality of this in the lives of believers is almost a fantasy; for most their lives are consumed with stress, anxiety, despair, and so forth, which are all spirits and attitudes that are contrary to a heavenly attitude of contentment.

The reality of heaven in the heart enables the child of God to endure even the severest of trials, but I must wonder how many attain to this level in our present age. The western culture in which we live is defined by seeking happiness and security through outward comfort. Excelling in the skill of outward comfort is merely to feed the passions of self-love deriving from the flesh. Thus, we wonder why we are always so discontented, when in fact we allow ourselves to be slaves to indwelling sin.

Throughout the Bible, God oftentimes restrains sin and its effects thereof in the lives of his children. In other cases like Romans 1 or in the second book of Thessalonians, he will not restrain sin as an act of judgment. Sometimes God, in his loving mercy, may take away an outward comfort like good relations with friends, reputation at work, or move us to an entirely different part of the country outside of our choosing. In other cases, the Lord, through his divine wisdom, may decide his child is not ready for a spouse, a promotion at work, or the healing of an affliction. In his sovereignty, he knows that if he were to bestow such a mercy, it would in the end destroy us. If I were to receive particular mercies before my heart was properly conditioned, it would consume me. Rather than being a blessing, it would be another affliction upon my soul.

The desire thereof does not derive from divine love, but from the sin principle still at work in my members. Therefore, the striving and seeking would be to satisfy the desires and passions of the flesh which only reap death and corruption upon the human soul. Certainly, there is no sin in seeking and desiring the mercies of God, but to seek them above all else as if our lives depended upon them is wrong. For God to remove an outward comfort or withhold the blessing of a particular mercy is for the overall objective of rooting out my sinful desires and conditioning my heart for himself.

It is terrible to be abandoned by God to the passions and desires of indwelling sin. As already stated, this is exactly what God does as a form of punishment upon those who forsake him. Moreover, if God decides its best that I should suffer the loss of such-and-such comfort or endure various trials, I shall yield and not rebel by complaining or crying out "Woe is me!" To have divine resources at work conditioning and fashioning my heart is to find God among the chaos. What a love gift from the King himself!

Whatever your affliction may be in effect could be ruining your life at this very moment. However, consider this: your heart has been under the reins and control of indwelling sin for so long that you don't even see it. The reality is your present mercies from God far outweigh your present afflictions—especially in our modern-day culture. If this were your very last day on earth, your afflictions would pale in comparison to the gift of salvation upon your soul, the sound health of your body, the ability to reason and think, the capability to breathe the life-sustaining air, and so forth. Oftentimes the afflictions we endure cloud our minds from the abundant mercies of God upon us. Which in turn also clouds our enjoyments from fellowship with God *in those mercies*. For we are commanded to rejoice always, pray without ceasing, and be thankful in all circumstances (1 Thessalonians 5:16-18), because there are inexpressible joy and unsurpassing peace found in doing so. However, if we are caught up in the afflictions of life, then it's all too easy to miss the blessings of heaven itself, or rather God himself in the midst of life.

Contentment comes from a proper understanding of God and his dispositions thereof in relation to the proper knowledge of self. In other words, to properly understand the corruption coming from within my own heart combined with proper knowledge of what God is actually doing in my life will produce the heavenly state of contentment.

The art of contentment is a skill that is constantly being trained and refined through everyday life. Paul learned this skill and was able, through the strength of Christ, to find contentment in any and every circumstance (Philippians 4:10-13). If you are able to learn this skill and find contentment in any and every circumstance despite your afflictions, indwelling sin, or any other external force for that matter, joy inexpressible will be the state of your soul. Greater glory will you bring to God's name; the composition of virtues active in the heart to produce such contentment like faith, hope, and love is great, to say the least.

The pursuit of the Son or rather the virtues of God will be addressed in further detail in the next chapter through the means of grace. Everything that has previously been addressed in this book will be brought together practically.

> *Dear Heavenly Father, thank you for your constant never-ending grace. Though sin may abound, your grace abounds all the more. The realities of indwelling sin and battle thereof may be great, yet your eternal love washes away all opposition. Father, keep our eyes and souls fixed on your Son, help us to pursue him above all else. In the pursuit thereof may your virtues reign supremely within our hearts, breathing life and contentment despite our circumstances. In times of darkness, help us to remember who we are in the life of your Son. Amen.*

CHAPTER 5

The Means of Grace

The means of grace is where everything begins to come together practically. Everything which has been addressed thus far—whether it be divine love, pursuing heaven in the heart, holiness, humility, the battle of indwelling sin, the art of contentment—can all be summed up in the pursuit of the Son through the means of grace. The means of grace are literally as they sound; they are means by which we have fellowship with and access to the grace of God. They are the avenues we all must take to partake in the fountain of life; without them it would be like trying to live without breathing.

God has bestowed upon his children many different means of grace as a gift; through them, we walk this earth in the presence of the Trinity. The primary three that Scripture emphasizes more than most are prayer, the Word of God, and meditation. The beauty of the three is that, like the Trinity, they intertwine together like a beautiful symphony. The child of God could solely focus on prayer alone or could be meditating upon the Word of God mixed with prayer. It's not uncommon to be reading the Word then immediately to transition to meditation based upon the Word itself, which can also easily lead to prayer with thanksgiving to God for his amazing glory.

Each of the three focuses is unique and special in its own way, for through them all, the child of God may have fellowship with God in this dance called life. Using the means of grace is much like an art; the more we seek the face of Christ through them, the more we fall in love with them. The more we fall in love with them, the more effective we become at using them individually, like a skilled painter we can gracefully paint a masterpiece using a variety of streams of life. In other words, the more skilled we are at using them, the more of God we will experience while in this life.

The Word of God

Mere words alone can never fully express the importance or beauty thereof of the Word of God. Thy Word is like a fire unto my soul; it is the very breath and life of every born-again believer. Through the Word we can see and behold the glory of the King, meaning that through God's Word, we see the character of God through Christ. His Word is his chosen means by which he reveals himself to man through his Spirit, as well as the means by which we also have fellowship with him. That's simply the beginning, for no external means can revive our souls; only God through his Word can do that (Psalm 19:7). As humility is an essential ingredient to the many virtues of God, the Word lays the foundation for every other means of grace, especially praying and meditation.

The Law of the L<small>ORD</small>

The Law of the L<small>ORD</small> is perfect, reviving the soul; the testimony of the L<small>ORD</small> is sure, making wise the simple; the precepts of the L<small>ORD</small> are right, rejoicing the heart; the commandment of the L<small>ORD</small> is pure, enlightening the eyes; the fear of the L<small>ORD</small> is clean enduring forever; the rules of the L<small>ORD</small> are true, and righteous altogether. More to be desired are they than gold, even much fine gold; sweeter also than honey and drippings of the honeycomb. Moreover, by them is your servant warned; in keeping them there is great reward. (Psalm 19:7-11)

God's Word is limitless in its importance and application to our lives. Through his Word we find divine wisdom that is not found in this world (19:7), the rejoicing of our hearts and understanding with discernment not found in ourselves (v. 8), eternal realities and truths that last forever (v. 9). One taste of God through his Word is like swimming in an ocean of life, leaving our souls longing and desiring for more. The more we swim, the more we desire and treasure his Word above all else in life (v. 10). The more acquainted we are with God through his Word, the more we are warned of the realities of sin and the ways of the world, thus walking in the ways of wisdom and finding great rewards as a result thereof (v. 11).

Though endless truths express the importance of the Word in our lives, two rise above the rest.

The Word Is the Unveiling of God's Glory

It has already been expressed and stated that God's virtues are the very life spring of our souls; by them we find purpose and life. Another way of stating this truth is that we were created by the glory of God *for the glory of God*. The glory of God, which is the external manifestation of his virtues, is where man can find true lasting and abiding peace of the heart. The Word is most essential in this pursuit, for only by the Word can we find the knowledge and understanding of these virtues. God's Word holds many purposes, but one of its primary functions is for the unveiling of God's glory. Moreover, the pursuit of many endeavors of the Christian life is entirely dependent upon the pursuit of the Son through his Word; or perhaps better stated, the pursuit of God's virtues within the human heart through his Word.

Your righteousness is righteous forever, and your law is true. (Psalm 119:142)

Righteousness is another word that can mean "right conduct." It is another term that is synonymous with "virtues, God's name, or his glory," all referring to the attributes of his character. It's many different ways of saying the same thing; the various definitions take on slightly different meanings on the surface, but they overlap each other at the core. All simply say that *righteousness* and *law* are directly connected in the sense that God's Word unveils his virtues or "righteousness."

The same truth is repeated by Paul when he says "love is the fulfilling of the law," which means God's Word or *law* is summed up by God's love. Its primary purpose is the unveiling of God's love, which is also the summation of his virtues (Romans 13:10). Simply stated, God's Word unveils his virtues or attributes.

David supports the truth that God's virtues are the very life springs of his soul, for he calls out to God asking the Lord to grant life to his soul according to God's Word: "Give me life according to your word!" (Psalm 119:25). David repeats the same truth later from a different angle: "In your steadfast love give me life" (119:88). Both requests refer to the life of God in the soul of man by his Spirit through his Word.

Beholding the Glory of God

Through the constant practice of reading the Word, memorizing the Word, and meditating upon the Word, the child of God will eventually behold the glory of God, thus in turn reflecting that glory in his own life. What a wonderful truth that the more of the beauty of God's glory you see through Scripture, the more you are conformed to those wonderful truths! (2 Corinthians 3:18). We live in an age where many see nothing but a disconnect between reading and doing. However, the truths of the Bible state that reading, which leads to meditation and understanding, *is doing*.

For instance, even from an unbiblical standpoint, it is well-known that convictions of the heart or rather living convictions are what produce or change external behavior. A person's behavior is merely the manifestation of his internal convictions; behavior is controlled and regulated by internal beliefs. For this reason, a constant study of the Word, which consist of daily reading, memorizing, and meditation is integral. By these means the Spirit produces life and change within our hearts. The more the eyes of our hearts are being enlightened to see God's glory (Ephesians 1:18), the more we are being transformed by God's glorious grace: "from one degree of glory to another" (2 Corinthians 3:18).

The child of God should be careful, nonetheless, not to deceive himself with thinking that having tremendous intellectual knowledge of the gospel will produce these truths. Having a plethora of knowledge of doctrine or Scripture does not necessarily mean one's heart has been changed by the Spirit. Knowledge that is not a practical knowledge is not true knowledge, but merely a person's exercise of deceiving himself into thinking he knows something. Practical knowledge or heart knowledge derives from memorizing; meditating upon God's Word night and day, daily prayer, and the experience gained from the fire of trials.

The idea of becoming the Word of God to the watching world is wonderfully illustrated by David:

> I have stored up your word in my heart, that I might not sin against you. (Psalm 119:11)

The believer's storing up God's Word within his heart literally means also storing up God's virtues within his soul. The more the child of God stores up, the more he will turn away from sin and walk in wisdom toward God and the watching world. In other words, the more the believer studies the Word of God, the more he will experience the realities of heaven in his heart. Christ himself confirms this truth in his prayer to his Father:

> Sanctify them in the truth; your word is truth. (John 17:17)

This singular verse contains so many marvelous truths! For man to be *sanctified* means to become holy or set apart for a specific purpose, namely, "in the truth" with truth referring to the very nature of God expressed through the words and commands of the Son. *"Your word"* refers to the sum total of the Word of God. Whether expressed through the prophets of old, Christ himself, or the apostles, all of Scripture is God-breathed and comes from God (2 Timothy 3:16). If the phrase *"is truth"* can refer to God's attributes, then another way of rendering this phrase could be *"Your word is life."* It could be as if Christ said:

> *Father, sanctify them in your word for your word contains life itself. Upon your word they shall be conformed into the image of your Son.*

*Upon your word shall they find virtues of life with
rivers of living water flowing richly within their
hearts. Upon your word they shall rise by faith
and walk in the way everlasting.*

The Word is our shield of faith against the rising waves of trials and afflictions, as well as our sword against the lies and assumptions that are asserted against us on a daily basis, whether from indwelling sin or from the world (Ephesians 6:16, 17). The Word is the source of everything that is relevant and practical to our lives, for by it we gain new understanding of ourselves and the world around us. The Word is the means by which our internal beliefs are forged and changed for the better. God's Word is a lamp unto our feet and our source of light in the darkness (Psalm 119:105). Through his Word we derive essential truths as to why we must suffer and how to rejoice in those sufferings. By his Word we come to realize that God will truly never leave us nor forsake us. Through his Word our eyes are opened to the reality of God's presence, and we can have fellowship with him through our everyday activities. If we are commanded to seek God's glory in all that we do (1 Corinthians 10:31), we may rest assured that God is also there at work for his glory (Romans 11:36). However, without God's Word, not one of these truths would ever be possible or attainable.

The Supremacy of the Word

The supremacy of the Word of life and God's divine nature are two themes repeated throughout Scripture. For instance, the entire chapter of 1 Corinthians 13 is devoted to the supremacy, importance, and nature of divine love. Spiritual gifts of great faith, working miracles, prophetic powers, or even the greatest acts of heroism mean nothing without divine love. The purpose of those gifts is for the exaltation of divine love. In the end they will pass away, but divine love will go on into eternity (1 Corinthians 13:8-10). Similarly, we see the same things applied to the supremacy of God's Word:

> For we did not follow cleverly devised myths when we made known to you the power and coming of our Lord Jesus Christ, but we were eyewitnesses of his majesty. For when he received honor and glory from God the Father, and the voice was borne to him by the Majestic Glory, "This is my beloved Son, with whom I am well pleased," we ourselves heard this very voice borne from heaven, for we were with him on the holy mountain. And we have the prophetic word more fully confirmed, to which you will do well to pay attention as to a lamp shining in a dark place, until the day dawns and the morning star rises in your hearts. (2 Peter 1:16-19)

Great and marvelous as those events were of seeing the glory of the Son unveiled right before their eyes and hearing the very voice of the majestic Father (vv. 16-18), the main purpose of those events was to solidify and exalt the Word. "And we have the prophetic word more fully confirmed...." The Word of God brings life and hope in times of darkness, 'tis the light of our hearts that should be sought after and guarded above all else. To do so will eventually result in the dawning of light upon our hearts and the rising of the morning star upon our souls (v. 19).

Meditation of the Soul

Meditation is the mind and heart being firmly fixed upon the truths of God revealed in Scripture. It's the practice of fixing our thoughts firmly upon a verse and digging deeper based upon the context or various key words. It's the art of seeing how one verse flows to the next or how one truth connects to another. Meditating upon the Word is the foundation; from there the child of God can meditate upon the beauties of God or compare his conduct to godly principles.

It is upon meditation that the Spirit deepens our understanding of God and ourselves, thus leading to a change in our practice. Meditation is one of the spiritual keys to finding life in the darkness and riding the storms of life, for we are unable to change the winds of adversity in life. Through meditation we can change our elevation and find a heavenly current. Through prayer combined with meditation, we can discern the circumstances of life and understand them from a godly perspective, thus producing peace and contentment of the heart.

Meditation, in general, allows the believer to dig deeper into the Word of God, learn more about God and his character, discover deeper understandings to biblical principles like holiness, produce new internal convictions, assess one's life in relation to biblical truth, and walk in deep fellowship with God as the heart and mind are fixed on the glories of Christ. This digging deeper is often performed with a combination of deep prayer and meditation. Meditating deeply upon a verse or biblical concepts can send the heart into a state of worship through prayer. The apostles did this in their own letters as they explained truth. Sometimes they became so excited they broke out into prayer mid-sentence, which is often referred to as a *doxology*. Paul had a habit of doing it anywhere and everywhere in his letters.

However, deepening our understanding of God all begins with first meditating upon his Word. Through meditating, the beauty and glory of Christ is applied to our hearts. As a result, our internal convictions are changed by the Spirit, which in turn changes our external practice.

The following examples of meditation are a select group of verses from daily reading and from meditation done throughout the day on memorized verses.

> Blessed is the man who walks not in the counsel of the wicked, nor stands in the way of sinners, nor sits in the seat of scoffers; but his delight is in the law of the Lord, and on his law he meditates day and night. He is like a tree planted by streams of water that yields its fruit in its season, and its leaf does not wither. In all that he does, he prospers. (Psalm 1:1-3)

The realities of verses 1 and 3 are entirely dependent upon the child of God's delighting in the law of the Lord and meditating upon his law day and night (v. 2). To not walk in the counsel of the wicked (v. 1) or to be like a tree firmly planted by the waters of life riding any storm that comes (v. 3) are fruits that spring forth from verse 2. In other words, meditation is the key of being anchored despite the winds of life (v. 3) and remaining unaffected from the ways of the world and the people of the world (v. 1).

Meditation from a Memory Verse

> Do nothing from selfish ambition or conceit, but in humility count others more significant than yourselves. (Philippians 2:3)

A normal face value reading of this verse would probably result in an individual's focusing on the behavior aspect of "do nothing from selfish ambition or conceit....." However, the key to this verse is the phrase "but in humility" Humility is the virtue that allows a person to count others more significant than himself, or to do nothing from his own interests or promote his external image on others (2:3). Understanding that humility is a proper understanding of myself in relation to God, which simply means: I'm a worm that's poor and destitute in spirit (Matthew 5:3) will enable me to have a proper disposition in relation to humility (Philippians 2:4). From there, the student of the Bible can branch off to the surrounding verses for further clarity. Verse 5 of Philippians 2 reveals that humility is a virtue upon my heart, but not because of myself. On the contrary, it's because I am one with Christ and found in him "which is yours in Christ Jesus." The example thereof of the humility of Christ is found in the illustration in verses 6-11.

To piece all of it together in relation to meditation means that meditating upon these truths should produce an understanding of the will through the Spirit that results in changed behavior. In other words, because I understand from the heart what humility is and how Christ portrayed that quality in his own life, I begin to analyze my own life to see how my conduct may or may not reflect that new understanding. Thus, my external behavior changes in order to reflect my new internal conviction given to me by the Spirit through meditation upon God's Word.

The Storm and the Disciples

One further example of meditation will be shown and illustrated through the life of Christ through the Gospels. Meditation in conjunction with correct study habits will illuminate the context of the passage, and with constant practice, the zealous student of the Bible will begin to see the depths of God's heart through any passage or verses:

On that day, when evening had come, he said to them, "Let us go across to the other side." And leaving the crowd, they took him with them in the boat, just as he was. And other boats were with him. And a great windstorm arose, and the waves were breaking into the boat, so that the boat was already filling. But he was in the stern, asleep on the cushion. And they woke him and said to him, "Teacher, do you not care that we are perishing?" And he awoke and rebuked the wind and said to the sea, "Peace! Be still!" And the wind ceased, and there was a great calm. He said to them, "Why are you so afraid? Have you still no faith?" And they were filled with great fear and said to one another, "Who then is this, that even the wind and the sea obey him?" (Mark 4:35-41)

To any student of Scripture, the story of Christ's calming the storm is quite familiar. The depths and riches of this particular passage are endless, but I shall endeavor to illuminate just a few.

As the end of a long day of teaching is coming to an end, Jesus so wisely wished to leave the crowds and pass on to another area (vv. 35, 36). However, all efforts to leave and find rest were met with an ensuring storm waiting for them over the horizon. Shortly thereafter, a "great windstorm arose" which caused the waves to arise which "...were breaking into the boat" (v. 37). While the disciples were beginning to fret and panic for their lives, Jesus was "...in the stern, asleep on the cushion" (v. 38).

I find some humor in this passage in the sense that the disciples are panicking for their lives while Jesus is sound asleep in the stern—like it's just another day in paradise. Their immediate response is a common, yet unsurprising, one: "Teacher, do you not care that we are perishing?" (v. 38). Though this story may pertain specifically to the disciples, their perception and response to the unfolding events is very common. How often does the child of God see the events of life unfolding around him and assume that God is asleep and does not care as the disciples felt when they questioned, "Do you not care that we are perishing?" (v. 38). Yet the Son's immediate response to quiet the raging storm and speak peace into life's circumstances reveals that he was in complete control the entire time (v. 39) and was merely testing them "…Why are you so afraid? Have you still no faith?" (v. 40).

A further look at the text shows that Jesus is essentially the eye of the storm; he was and is the heart of it all. He was the calm before the storm, during the storm "asleep on the cushion," (v. 38), and after the storm,"the wind ceased, and there was a great calm" (v. 39). The essential principles revealed from this passage show that no matter what the storms of life may be, Christ is the center of it all. The storms of life are within his sovereign purposes, and they will end when his purposes have been fulfilled. He does not leave his children to be blown to and fro by them; rather, in his sovereignty he allows them to take place. Thereby is the believers' faith *in him* strengthened, and in the coming storms, they may find rest in him, as he is the eye of the storm.

Purposes of Meditation

The Word is the means by which God's glory (his virtues) is expressed with meditation being the avenue of which we can understand and apply God's Word to our own lives. Without the Word, meditation would be an exercise of futility; however, without meditation the believer could not learn about spiritual truths or apply them to his own life. In addition to God's Word, meditation is one of the greatest gifts given to us by God. Through meditation upon the Word, the Christian can find an anchor for his soul despite the storm encircling him. Through this art the Christian learns to be like a tree planted by rivers of life that yield eternal fruit which can never pass away.

Self-Examination of the Heart

Meditation upon God's Word itself can also lead the Christian to examine his own soul. Every Christian should ask himself: does my life and my conduct reflect God in such a way that is worthy of his name or bring delight to his heart? Questions like this should be in the back of the believer's mind on a daily basis. David wonderfully illustrates this truth:

> Search me, O God, and know my heart! Try me and know my thoughts! And see if there be any grievous way in me, and lead me in the way everlasting! (Psalm 139:23, 24)

Many verses illustrate this truth, but this one rises above the rest because it expresses so many marvelous truths. The first truth expressed is that God searches our heart. "Search me, O God, and know my heart." Who better to search our heart than God himself? This is where meditation, prayer, and the Word become essential to each other. Godly self-examination requires meditation through prayer based upon the Word. In other words, because God searches our heart—not we ourselves—prayer becomes essential. Prayer is the means by which the soul enters into communion and fellowship with God. Meditation with prayer allows every Christian to examine his own soul with God bringing things to the believer's mind by his Spirit through his Word.

Self-examination should always be done with God in prayer. Doing so outside of him can easily result in overwhelming despair and sorrow of the heart or result in the believer's self-reliance of trying to fix himself. In any case, looking to self is not the appropriate source to which a person should look. At the core of feeling overwhelming despair over one's actions is actually pride in some cases. Because "I" didn't perform well enough, despair springs forth from the belief that's centered on self and not God.

The reality should be "I'm a creation of God created for his glory." Therefore, the gifts and abilities we have are ultimately from God (1 Corinthians 4:7), thus we truly are dependent upon him. This same truth can be applied to self-improvement that stems from a view of self-reliance. Which in turn will only repeat the cycle of guilt, shame, convictions to change, acts of atonement to carry it out, and ending in failure. True change and self-examination are dependent upon the Lord, not ourselves.

Looking to God to be the one to "see if there be any grievous way in me" (as we should) will result in brokenness over sin. That brokenness will then lead to the healing of the heart as God removes entangling sins and breathes grace upon the soul, thus finding comfort that relies upon the Lord and not ourselves (Matthew 5:4). To enter into self-examination with God will ultimately result in being led in the way eternal, "in the way everlasting!" (Psalm 139:24).

Practical Implications

A practical implication of these truths can be seen in everyday life. For instance, becoming impatient or losing your temper at a long line in a restaurant or a traffic jam is not simply a sinful attitude toward others you do not know; in truth, its an act of pride against God and his providence (Philippians 2:13-15). The providential purpose behind those events could be for the promotion of humility and godliness upon your heart or perhaps a chance given to you by God to cast your anxieties and angers upon him through prayer and not the next person who crosses your path—like your significant other (1 Peter 5:6, 7).

Having God's Word stored in your heart will enable your conscience to come down like a hammer when you act contrary to what you know is right. In the case of losing patience because of traffic or long lines, you should take a mental note and bring it to God during a time that is dedicated toward deep prayer. A key consideration for those prayer times is keeping in mind you will not truly repent or change unless you are repenting over the sin itself—not the consequences of sin. For example, I may act out of anger toward a fellow Christian and grieve in my heart for the way I hurt that person and strained our relationship. I will go before God in prayer and ask for mercy to restore our relationship which he may answer, according to divine wisdom. However, if my concern is more focused on the effects of sin and not the sin itself, I will only repeat the deed at another time.

True biblical repentance is more concerned with the sin itself in relation to God. Such was the case with David when he sinned against Bath-sheba, though he committed adultery and sanctioned the death of her husband Uriah (2 Samuel 11:14, 15). David was more brokenhearted over the fact that he had sinned against God (Psalm 51:4), thus he was able to turn away from sin. Repentance is the turning away from sin that derives from a broken spirit over sin in relation to God. Regret is grief over the consequences and effects of sin—not so much sin itself. The primary consideration should be over sin itself; the secondary consideration is over the effects and consequences of sin. Both have their proper place with due considerations.

To bring this explanation all together in relation to self-examination with God, the child of God should bring forth matters to his Heavenly Father in prayer with a heart of brokenness and contrition. If you are anything like me, sometimes I have a hard time conjuring an attitude of brokenness because I love my sin. Therefore, I ask God to break my heart over the things that break his. As a result, I begin to ponder and meditate upon the truths of the Word and ask questions like: "Why are my actions ungodly and wrong?" I can only say that the revelations which come to mind from meditation can be startling, to say the least. To act out in selfish anger against my fellow Christian not only breaks the heart of God (Ephesians 4:30), but it is also to act out of my own standards of selfishness, thus judging God's law of love and ultimately judging God himself (cf. James 4:11–12).

Such a revelation will ultimately produce brokenness within the heart and lead to an understanding that produces wisdom to avoid such beliefs and behaviors. Further meditation through prayer with God will lead to new understandings that enable us to place godly convictions into practice. For example, knowing the truth behind impatience and discontentment toward God in relation to traffic jams will cause us to avoid such behavior and instead to respond humbly with meekness. Such is the only proper conduct toward a loving God who gave everything for us. These examples are only some of the means the Spirit uses to change our hearts and to bring about more Christlikeness. Though meditation involves a great deal of action and responsibility on our end, nevertheless, it is God who is at work in our hearts both to will and work for his good pleasure (Philippians 2:13).

Indeed, in addition to his Word, meditation is one of the greatest gifts given to us by God. Through meditation upon the Word, an anchor can be found for the believer's soul despite the ensuing storm around him. Through this art the Christian learns to be like a tree planted by rivers of life that yield eternal fruit that can never pass away.

Prayer, the Art of Spiritual Breathing

Prayer is one of the most essential components to the Christian life; it's the art of spiritual breathing. Just as breathing is essential to the human body for survival, so is prayer to the human soul. Prayer is the means by which our souls commune and fellowship with God; it's also how the believer may enter into the throne room of God, finding mercy and grace to help in time of need (Hebrews 4:16). Through prayer the Word is applied to our lives intertwined with meditation; however, without prayer the other two cannot function. By prayer the believer may seek the will of the Lord and ask anything in accordance with his will, knowing he will hear and grant such requests by faith (1 John 5:14–15; Matthew 21:22). Such knowledge produces stronger faith and an acute sense of God's presence which brings the soul in closer intimacy with the majestic Trinity.

The stronger our knowledge of the Word is mixed with daily meditation throughout the day, the more of a thriving prayer life the child of God will have. Each grace contributes to the other; if one is thriving then all should be thriving. The uniqueness of the means of grace functions very similarly to the Trinity: If one member of the Trinity is involved in something, then all three are involved in some way. This same truth applies to the Word, meditation, and prayer; where one is involved, all three are usually involved.

Prayer can be simply broken down as the art of seeking the Lord's presence and conversing with him with a humble heart based upon the Word. The Word lays the foundation for my knowledge and understanding of God, which influences my requests and conversations with him daily. For instance, the Word tells me to pray without ceasing (1 Thessalonians 5:17), how to pray (Luke 11:2-4), to seek God boldly as my intimate Heavenly Father (Romans 8:15; Luke 18:7), that we may ask him the desires of our heart, seek it with all of our might, and find the door opened in his timing (Matthew 7:7, 8), but if we do not ask, we will never have or obtain the desires of our hearts like the salvation of a lost family member (James 4:2).

There are two major elements or forms of prayer. Intentional times of prayer are times set aside to have deep prayer and fellowship with God. The other form is continuous prayer that is performed throughout the day; it's more like a continuous conversation with God that has no real end.

Intentional Prayer

Times of intentional or deep prayer take place when the child of God purposely gets away from everyone and everything in order to converse with his Heavenly Father. Jesus was arguably the busiest person on the earth during his three-year ministry; at times he had multitudes of crowds gathering to hear his teachings and to be physically healed:

> But now even more the report about him went abroad and great crowds gathered to hear him and to be healed of their infirmities. But he would withdraw to desolate places and pray. (Luke 5:15–16)

Instead of engaging what could be considered the peak of such a ministry with countless crowds, Christ intentionally withdrew from everyone: "to desolate places and pray" (v. 16). In today's culture the more active a person is, the more productive he is believed to be. However, such was not the case with Christ; by his actions, he made a loud statement that time with his Heavenly Father supersedes everything else. Christ set the pattern for how the Christian is supposed to live in this life and to seek God above all else (1 Peter 2:21), and he accomplished that goal by placing a higher priority on fellowship with God above possibly the apex of his ministry at the time (Luke 5:15–16). Christ's example confirms the command to seek God and his righteousness above all else, and everything else shall be added to us (Matthew 6:33).

In other words, to set aside time despite what may be going on in life for God enables the accomplishment of everything else in life. Since it is God who works all things according to the counsel of his own will (Ephesians 1:11), and so by seeking him in deep prayer (intentional prayer) one can find the strength, wisdom, and the endurance to do the impossible. To place a higher priority on the tasks and responsibilities of life above God is to walk by sight and not by faith. It's to engage everything in life by one's own strength—not the strength that God lavishly supplies by faith. Instead of walking in the glory of heaven, one is actually, in effect, walking in the weight of sin that breathes trouble and sorrows upon the soul.

Its during times of deep prayer that the anxieties of life can be brought forth before him who sits upon heaven's throne; who delights in exchanging death for life, sorrow for joy, or in this particular case, anxiety for peace. These are the times the child of God can empty his heart before God and allow the Spirit of life to clothe him with humility and align his will with the will of God (1 Peter 5:6, 7). Intentional prayer is a time the Christian may go into self-examination with God, for deep prayer allows the soul of man to intertwine with the Spirit of God and produce living convictions.

The Spirit himself is the source of our prayer (Ephesians 6:18), he is also our teacher through the Word (1 John 2:27). Deep prayer is the time for meditation with self-examination in regard to discerning the Lord's will for various situations or as a time to repent over our conduct in life. Through deep prayer the Spirit is our helper by aiding the faculties of our soul, which consist of the Spirit's applying biblical principles and truths to our thoughts, wills, and emotions, thus producing new understandings or various discernments.

Intentional prayer is what I like to refer as times of heaven in the heart. It is the very act of the soul's having fellowship with God the Father through the intercession of the Son with the Spirit's breathing our hearts into a spring of life. The heart of man becomes fashioned by God himself to resemble the beauty of the gardens of heaven and the realities of God's glory.

Deep prayer is a discipline that should be practiced by every Christian. Throughout the Gospels, Christ is often seen retreating to desolate places to pray, which emphasizes its importance because none of us are sinless. Some set aside time every day for intentional prayer which is a great practice. The habit of getting away once a week for at least an hour to converse with God in deep prayer is life changing, and ultimately breath taking. Some habits formed in this life will carry over into eternity, so we might as well start now.

Continuous Prayer, the Art of Conversing with God

Continuous prayer is the art and practice of conversing with God throughout the day. It is not a sophisticated formal prayer that only the religious elite perform. On the contrary, it is the act of constant fellowship and conversation with God the Father. It's the believer's practice of praying verbally out loud or internally within his own mind. Most individuals who become Christians instinctively begin to pray about anything and everything—like a newborn who instinctively knows how to breathe from the moment of birth.

Praying without ceasing is a command that is often repeated throughout Scripture:

> Do not be anxious about anything, but in everything by prayer and supplication with thanksgiving let your requests be made known to God. (Philippians 4:6)

Continuous prayer is a wonderful gift from God to man, for by it we may walk this life with God right by our side. It is the bridge between the soul of man and the throne of grace. Engaging the Lord "in everything" can range from cooking breakfast in the morning to asking for help to present the gospel to a lost soul. In doing so, the anxieties and burdens of this life are placed upon the shoulders of Christ who delights in dispensing grace. Engaging in continuous prayer is the only way to carry out the command, "Do not be anxious about anything." Only by talking with the Lord consistently do we remember who we are in Christ and walk in the realities of grace.

Through constant or unending prayer the child of God may see the physical world through a spiritual lens. Although the Word and meditation lay the foundation for having an intimate awareness of God's presence throughout the day, constant prayer fuels an ongoing awareness of the Lord's presence and allows the believer to reason with his own soul. For example, instead of losing our cool due to unfair treatment from slander or illwill, praying in that very moment for strength can have incomprehensible effects. It's the quilivant of going before the throne of grace with confidence and thus finding mercy and grace to help in our time of need (Hebrews 4:16). In other words, it's the physical act of the soul going before God for help, and thus the Lord exchanges the anger and bitterness in the heart with humility and peace that surpasses all understanding.

Such acts bring an immediate awareness and remembrance of the Lord's presence, thus flooding the mind with practical spiritual truths (which comes from constant study and meditation). In conjunction, understanding truths that the righteous are bound for many afflictions in life (Psalm 34:19), like that of unfair treatment, testing circumstances, and the like, produces humility that quenches pride from within. Other truths that may come to mind include the fact that Christ walked the same path and experienced far worse. Moreover, that we deserve such treatments, but Christ never deserved them; his experiences far outweigh anything we could ever experience. Constant prayer can bring unending fellowship with Christ and safeguard the soul from the ultimate effects of external circumstances.

In the next chapter, practical steps and examples of developing these gifts as habits will be addressed more in depth. From there, the chapter will transition to what those habits could look like daily and how that produces spiritual stability in a believer's life.

> *Dear Heavenly Father, thank you for your steadfast love deriving from your dearly beloved Son. In a world where things are always amiss and afflictions are nothing but guaranteed, you have given us life through the means of grace. Your gracious gifts are the means by which we may experience heaven upon the heart and enjoy fellowship with your Son. Thank You for such heavenly gifts, please deepen our understanding of them and apply them to our hearts. May our souls be steadfast in keeping them and seeking your heart through them. Amen.*

CHAPTER 6

Spiritual Stability Through the Means of Grace

Spiritual stability through the means of grace is ultimately one of the most practical foundations that should be sought by every Christian. Having an intimate and rich understanding of each means of grace lays the foundation for applying them in life. For without understanding there can be no lasting life change.

The last chapter is dedicated to defining the various means of grace and understanding them so they can be applied practically. From here we transition to developing such godly understandings into everyday life habits. Ultimately, over time, adopting these daily habits will produce spiritual stability in the life of a believer.

To embark upon this journey its helpful to know that the means of grace function very similarly to the nature of the Trinity and God's attributes. The beauty of the three members of the Trinity is their constant communion and fellowship with one another. The Trinity always works together for the common goal of the emanation of God's glory. In the similar manner, the nature of God's attributes and the means of grace always work in cohesion and overlap each other. For example, faith and hope overlap and function in unison; yet without divine love, they would have no foundation. In a like manner, God's Word is the foundation with prayer and meditation functioning in unison together with dependence upon the Word. Seeking the Lord and his kingdom above all else rises or falls based upon these foundational gifts from God.

A life that is filled with daily habits of reading the Bible, meditating, and praying is a life that is filled with the realities of heaven. Those who have the Spirit of Christ within them can have a foretaste of heaven—if their life is based upon these foundational truths. Developing habits that are centered on the means of grace mixed with proper planning can have life-changing effects upon a Christian's life. Everyone's walk with Christ and circumstances in life will vary from person to person. The following points are meant to be guides that will help develop daily habits based upon these graces:

Devotional Times

Establishing a certain time each and every single time for God and God alone is a wise practice. Throughout the Gospels, Christ is known for dropping everything and placing a higher priority with spending time with God:

> And rising very early in the morning while it
> was still dark, he departed and went to a desolate
> place, and there he prayed. (Mark 1:35)

Whether it was rising early or spending time at night, Christ was always spending time with his Father. In either case, wisdom suggests having an allotted time—whether it is 30 minutes or two hours—having that time each day for God is extremely beneficial.

During this time one can find daily grace to fuel his heart for the day. Normal everyday life is a spiritual battlefield for every Christian; therefore, putting on armor before the daily battle begins is a wise habit (Ephesians 6:10-18). Every child of God can develop daily habits of reading, praying, and meditating early in the morning that will mend the soul with grace. These daily habits help center the mind on Christ and flood the heart with life. The soul of man becomes infused with the very life of God that is armor against life's daily stress and burdens. Indeed, everyone's circumstances are different, so for some, the best time for these daily disciplines may be in the evening prior to falling asleep. In either case, simply setting aside dedicated time, daily for a mixture of daily reading, prayer, and meditation is most refreshing for the soul.

Through these habits life changes begin to happen. Setting aside dedicated time in the morning or in the evening right before bed are two optimal times. Some develop habits of both with a primary emphasis on the morning and a smaller amount of time, possibly 15-30 minutes, at night. Adopting a nighttime means of grace allows an individual to place his burdens and anxieties on Christ, which paves the way for graceful sleep. There is wisdom for either time period; my prayer and hope simply is that one of those times becomes dedicated for daily reading, prayer, and meditation in every Christian's life.

The Daily Reading of the Word

Dedicated time for the Lord daily allows sufficient time for reading the Word. Reading God's Word is essential to laying the foundation for all of the other means of grace. The first matter to consider is to have some type of reading plan. Without it, the quality of reading may diminish and begin to waver over time. Various reading plans can range from basic plans like reading four chapters a day to reading through the entire Bible in a year, to more complex plans that consist of memorization, as well as reading in both the Gospels and the Old Testament. For example, choosing to read four chapters a day breaks down the discipline as follows: one chapter is dedicated to memorization and meditation for extensive quality reading, two chapters dedicated to reading systematically through the Old Testament, and one chapter in the Gospels dedicated to reading through Matthew, Mark, Luke, and John. Plans will vary; nonetheless, it is extremely wise to read God's Word daily with some sort of plan.

Memorizing the Word

Memorizing God's Word is an essential tool that aids the art of prayer and meditation. The importance of memorization is emphasized beginning in Deuteronomy:

> You shall therefore lay up these words of mine in your heart and in your soul, and you shall bind them as a sign on your hand and they shall be as frontlets between your eyes. (Deuteronomy 11:18)

It continues to be repeated throughout the New Testament that believers should let the Word of Christ dwell in them richly (Colossians 3:16). The principle is essential and vital as it provides fuel for the other means of grace to operate. Meditation and continuous prayer would be hindered severely if God's Word wasn't stored within the heart as a basis to provide thoughts for meditation or desires for prayer (Psalm 119:11). It would be like trying to prolong a fire without adding additional wood as a fuel source.

For the person who is unaccustomed to memorization, it can be a struggle at first. However, with anything new it takes effort and repetition, with that it becomes more natural over the course of time. Starting the memorization process can include silently reading a particular verse or out loud as many as twenty times, then repeating it mentally ten to twenty times without looking at the verse. Memorizing the verse in sections can be very helpful. With consistent practice, memorizing verses can take no more than five minutes. Repeating the verse throughout the day and meditating upon it will help retain and solidify it in the mind.

Daily Meditation

Daily meditation is another vital element to help establish spiritual stability and for laying the foundation in life. Meditation is yet another principle emphasized throughout Scripture. Interestingly enough, many are familiar with the following verse: "Have I not commanded you? Be strong and courageous. Do not be frightened, and do not be dismayed, for the LORD your God is with you wherever you go" (Joshua 1:9). Many memorize this famous verse to find courage and strength in times of need. However, it's also vital to take into account the preceding verse:

> This book of the law shall not depart from your mouth, but you shall meditate on it day and night, so that you may be careful to do according to all that is written in it. For then you will make your way prosperous, and then you will have good success. (Joshua 1:8)

Meditation upon "the book of the law" is simply the Word of God. So meditation upon the Word is the necessary element to making "your way prosperous" or having "good success." It is also the vital link establishing the grounds of verse 9 to "be strong and courageous" and being aware of the Lord's presence, "for the

Lᴏʀᴅ your God is with you wherever you go." Without meditation, it is impossible to carry out these commands, the command to be strong and courageous and overcome overwhelming odds through the Lord's strength is possibly only through meditation upon his Word. This truth is emphasized in the beginning of the verse, "you shall meditate on it day and night, so that you may be careful to do according to all that is written in it" (v. 8). The word "For" is to illustrate the point or give the why behind meditation, which in this case is "to make your way prosperous", and "you will have good success". The same principle is also the key to verse 9.

Daily meditation upon the Word through daily reading is one way to meditate. Choosing a specific chapter or key verses in a daily reading plan can provide deeper quality reading. Meditating upon memorization verses is also another vital practice that allows meditation throughout the day. Meditation is the believer's means of discovering more of the heart of God and the bridge to applying those realties to life; it is how one can make discernments about certain situations and use godly wisdom to navigate them. Whether its digging deeper into God's Word, getting lost in deep prayer, or meditating upon the Word, all of these result in the soul having fellowship with Christ through everyday life.

Meditation can be done during devotional times. Meditation, in general, has many purposes and can be used in a variety of ways to seek and glorify God. It should be done during devotional times and continued throughout the day during down times. For example, any type of car ride like the commute to work, plane rides, waiting in lines, folding clothes, doing dishes, or anytime you are walking to a destination are examples of times that can be used for meditation. Though some people may be genuinely unable to meditate during those times, another consideration is this: if you find your mind wandering due to boredom or daydreaming about this and that, you have discovered a great time to meditate upon eternal realities that yield eternal benefit.

Daily Prayer

As I have already stated, prayer for the Christian is like breathing. The hand of God can often be seen moving through the prayers of his saints. Intentional and continuous prayer should be daily habits like eating and putting on clothes. Intentional prayer is planned prayer that can be done during a believer's devotional times for ten to fifteen minutes or even longer, time permitting. Praying for certain people, events of the day, daily grace, and the like can be done during this time. Planned prayer is the initial setting of the fire with continuous prayer throughout the day fueling it.

Continuous prayer shares the same rules of meditation. It can be done whenever time permits. Praying without ceasing throughout the day keeps the heart in sync with grace and allows the soul to walk in heavenly fellowship with God (Philippians 4:6). Through any and every circumstance in life, continuous prayer allows the soul to refocus with a godly perspective, thus finding God in the darkest corners of life.

Self-Examination with Deep Prayer

As stated earlier, self-examination is extremely beneficial but should only be done with God in prayer. Engaging upon deep prayer with an emphasis on self-examination can be done so once a week. An hour would certainly suffice, but more time is always encouraged, if possible.

To view self-examination lightly could prove to be costly. For instance, Christ says, "For everyone who exalts himself will be humbled, and he who humbles himself will be exalted" (Luke 14:11). The natural disposition of our hearts is to walk in pride and not in humility; therefore, self-examination is an essential gift given to us all. Through it, we may humble ourselves, but to disregard it will result in the Lord humbling us himself:

> But if we judged ourselves truly, we would not be judged. But when we are judged by the Lord, we are disciplined so that we may not be condemned along with the world (1 Corinthians 11:31–32).

To bring our faults, flaws, anxieties, and sorrows of this life to God will not only avoid the humbling hand of the Almighty. It will also bring healing to our souls as he clothes us with grace and exalts us in his majesty.

Bringing It All Together

A practical approach to applying all of the various means of grace to life starts with establishing a devotional time. Whether that time is first thing in the morning or at nighttime, it should incorporate daily reading of the Word, meditation, planned prayer times, and Bible memorization. Devotional times are the initial step of igniting the heart with grace, with continuous prayer and meditation being the means by which the fire continues to burn brightly.

Some of the means of grace can be done during devotional times and continued afterward throughout the day. The one who prays without ceasing and meditates night and day can walk with God and consistently seek his glory. Devotional times start the fire while endless prayer with meditation fuels the fire and keeps it burning. The more a Christian is consistent in these graces, the stronger the fire will be. In addition, scheduling in some time once a week for deep prayer with self-examination will solidify the foundational habits for a godly life.

The Life of a Stable Soul

A soul that is not spiritually stable in Christ will be blown to and fro by the winds of prosperity and adversity. However, a believer's life that is defined by these habits of grace will look entirely different. A heart that is infused with the life of God through the means of grace allows an intimate awareness of God's presence and fellowship with him through the activities of everyday life. Furthermore, spiritual stability of the soul is not absent of reality and the trials of everyday life. In fact, if the soul is stable then so is the mind and judgments regarding the circumstances in life, which carries over to the will and emotions. Spiritual stability encorporates not just the spiritual aspect of life but also the physical, it encompasses every dimension of life.

The art of seeking Christ above all else through the means of grace has many profound practical realities for every believer. Philippians 4:1-13 comprehensively covers these truths in addition to many other practical realities that are a result of such practices.

The Bond of Peace Through Love

Therefore, my brothers, whom I love and long for, my joy and crown, stand firm thus in the Lord, my beloved. I entreat Euodia and I entreat Syntyche to agree in the Lord. Yes, I ask you also, true companion, help these women, who have labored side by side with me in the gospel together with Clement and the rest of my fellow workers, whose names are in the book of life. (Philippians 4:1–3.

At this point in Paul's letter to the Philippians, the apostle is encouraging and commanding the Philippians to "stand firm thus in the Lord" (v. 1), which is the equivalent of having the soul rooted and grounded in Christ. In other words, it's the transition and exhortation to be spiritually stable in life through the appointed means which God has designed.

Of all of the different ways with which Paul could start to carry out the command "stand firm thus in the Lord," he takes a very unique and interesting path. He takes the approach of encouraging two sisters to stop their conflict with one another and to "agree in the Lord" (v. 2). He reaches out to a dear friend "true companion" known as "loyal Syzygus" to help with the reconciliation process. The question is raised as to why would Paul start with this? Why call them out openly in a letter like that?

Quite simply, Paul knew the heart of the matter and wisely approached it. He knew the prominence of those two women within the church, and he knew their conflict was causing division. He knew that spiritual stability begins with the bond of peace through love. Their rivalry was destroying that very core principle, which is why he openly called them out and addressed the issue. Seeking the bond of peace through love is vital and integral for everything else to flow forth. Love as addressed earlier is the core from which all the other graces or virtues operate. Without love anyone could have all faith as to move mountains with prophetic powers, but it would all be for nothing (1 Corinthians 13:1–3).

Therefore, love is the essential foundation that must be in place for everything else to work properly. The bond of peace driven by love is to seek the well-being and joy of all those around within the glory of God. It means being willing to make hard choices or call out various individuals for their actions like Paul did for the sake of everyone else. Every circumstance will vary and always warrants a different response, but an individual whose heart is driven by love through the means of grace to seek Christ and his glory is well on the path to finding stability of the soul.

The Art of Rejoicing

Rejoice in the Lord always; again I will say, rejoice. (Philippians 4:4)

The joy of the Lord is our strength in this life (Nehemiah 8:10). The very eternal joy that flows between the Father and the Son is given to every believer as a gift (John 17:13). It is the joy of heaven upon the heart. The beauty of such a gift and command to rejoice always is that the command is not dependent or based upon our circumstances. On the contrary, it is the result of a life that is defined by the means of grace and a heart that is inflamed with love from above. The child of God can rejoice and abound in inexpressible joy because the source of such joy is the Lord himself: "in the Lord." *Rejoicing* in the Lord means to delight in God's character and everything that he does.

The means of grace are the very fuel source for rejoicing in the Lord always. Only through the Word, unceasing prayer, and ever-constant meditation can one's eyes be opened to God's presence. Having an intimate awareness of God's presence sends the soul straight into the heart of the Father. We know that we are not alone in our current endeavors, for the majestic Trinity is ever-present and working in every circumstance according to the counsel of his own will for our good and his glory, which will bring heavenly joy to any soul.

Perhaps you or someone that you know is presently experiencing some of the worst circumstances in life with no hope of joy on the horizon; and the very prospect of finding joy let alone presently rejoicing brings nothing but sheer anger and more sorrow. For that reason I cannot and will not appeal to myself for answers or pretend to know how to handle what you or your friend may be going through. However, I know that there are some, namely Paul, who manged to find joy and contentment even in the midst of some of life's worst trials (Acts 16:25).

Ultimately, it is unavoidable and inevitable that we will be brought down by the sorrows of this life; however, even then our joy can be and should be ever-constant in the Lord (2 Corinthians 6:10). The joy of meditating upon God's virtues revealed in Scripture or seeing his faithfulness firsthand is evidence of a stable soul. Experiencing a duality of sorrow and joy may be a paradox, nevertheless it's still a reality.

The Presence of God

> Let your reasonableness be known to everyone. The Lord is at hand; do not be anxious about anything, but in everything by prayer and supplication with thanksgiving let your requests be made known to God. And the peace of God, which surpasses all understanding, will guard your hearts and your minds in Christ Jesus. (Philippians 4:5–7)

The fruits of a stable soul are further exemplified in a heart that is driven by humility leading to gracious words and acts of love to all (v. 5). The word *reasonableness* has contained within it the idea of "mercy, humility, graciousness, kindness," and the like. In other words, because the heart is filled with joy from a Savior who gave everything for our sakes, our conduct toward others is a reflection or byproduct of that joy. Love to God naturally overflows into our relations and conduct with others. The joy that comes from God's love (v. 4) overflows directly into our interactions with everyone else in our life (v. 5).

Its through prayer that one enters the heart of God and thereby is able to cast his anxieties upon his Heavenly Father. "…Do not be anxious about anything, but in everything by prayer and supplication…" (v. 6). Anxiety is the result of a weary soul's acting according to its own strength and limited resources, rather than working with God. Working with God through the rest that he provides (cf. Matthew 11:28–30; Hebrews 4), is always stronger and more beneicial than trying to work for God in one's own strength. For through endless prayer, one is able to cast his anxieties onto God and exchange restlessness for the peace of God (v. 7), thus finding rest for his weary soul in Christ (Matthew 11:28, 29). However, only through consistent prayer that begins at the rising of the sun and continues to the dawning of the stars at night can this be done. "…but in everything by prayer and supplication…" (v. 6).

The moment the we stop praying and meditating upon the Word of God, is the moment the soul becomes distracted with the worries of this life, accumulating sorrows and anxieties. We forget that Christ carried our sorrows and griefs at the cross (Isaiah 53:4); through prayer, Christ takes those from us and bestows his benevolent peace upon our hearts. In doing so, the peace of God which "…will guard your hearts and your minds in Christ Jesus" (v. 7), opens our eyes to being conscientious of God's presence and his work of providence: "The Lord is at hand…" (v. 5). As a result, we no longer see life through a limited narrow view of physical realities; rather, we begin to see as God sees, which is the physical realm through the spiritual. We begin to see and live by faith and not by sight alone.

It's to see the events and circumstances of life in connection with spiritual truths and not limited to the physical alone. Perception of life changes drastically; no longer is things viewed or marked off as "coincidence", the very understanding of life and why certain things happen is no longer based upon human reason alone. For instance, an individual may be persecuted and treated unfairly by another, which he acknowledges is happening because of that individual's choice. However, he also acknowledges that God, in his sovereignty, is allowing it to happen for the purpose of promoting humility in the heart, and because we are destined to walk the same path of glory through suffering which Christ himself walked (1 Peter 2:21; Philippians 1:29).

The soul is rather in tune with the heart of the Father and the work of his hand through providence. It's as if God bestows spiritual eyes upon the individual, for they can now sense the Lord's presence and sense his work of glory through the natural events of life. Every event or circumstance in some way expresses God's glorious virtues; the more the believer is in tune with the heart of God, the more he will see.

Walking in fellowship with God through the means of grace can transform a weary soul burdened by the sorrows of this life into a spring of life echoing the beauties of the gardens of God. The heart is filled with peace that surpasses all understanding and the very joy of the Son, which is inexpressible and filled with glory. The soul walks in fellowship with the Trinity and experiences the realities of heaven. Such grace overflows the heart with awe and wonder. The soul is now a tree planted by rivers of living water, still experiencing the winds of affliction and storms of life; yet is firmly rooted and grounded by the riverside, bearing fruits of life and grace—despite the external conditions.

Thoughts of Excellence

Finally, brothers, whatever is true, whatever is honorable, whatever is just, whatever is pure, whatever is lovely, whatever is commendable, if there is any excellence, if there is anything worthy of praise, think about these things. What you have learned and received and heard and seen in me— practice these things, and the God of peace will be with you. (Philippians 4:8–9)

Paul is now moving into his final exhortation which transitions to the importance of meditation (v. 8). Ultimately, all godly thoughts for meditation derive ultimately from the Word. The meditation of the mind—"think about these things"—that is centered on anything godly "whatever is lovely", or excellent "if there is any excellence", and so forth, lays the foundation for all of the previous commands. It's the reason Paul chose to list it last, "Finally" and why he covers it extensively and so comprehensively. The thoughts of the heart determine the actions of an individual. If the soul is infused with thoughts that are honorable, just, pure, lovely, and the like, it provides the necessary framework for the heart to be driven by godly love. Love is the foundation and starting principle in verses 1–3; from there, love overflows like a domino effect, enabling one to rejoice always (v. 4) and pray in everything (v. 6).

The culmination of all of these practices, "practice these things" will result not only in supernatural joy and peace, but the God of peace himself residing within the heart, "and the God of peace will be with you" (v. 9).

Heavenly Contentment

I rejoiced in the Lord greatly that now at length you have revived your concern for me, but you had no opportunity. Not that I am speaking of being in need, for I have learned in whatever situation I am to be content. I know how to be brought low, and I know how to abound. In any and every circumstance, I have learned the secret of facing plenty and hunger, abundance and need. I can do all things through him who strengthens me. (Philippians 4:10–13)

If the God of peace is reigning and ruling from within (v. 9), than the inevitable result is the contentment of the soul (v. 11). Paul is able to rejoice and abound in any and every circumstance because his heart is overflowing with the virtues of grace. The soul naturally clings to this world and circumstance to find contentment. The strength of a Christian lies in the art of finding heavenly contentment despite one's circumstances. Paul practiced what he preached and learned through experience, "I know how to be brought low, and I know how to abound", how to find contentment in God and God alone. Poverty at times can be one of the greatest gifts from God to man, for the soul is unable to cling to the corruption of this world. As a result, the heart is left with the only option of riding the waves of faith into the heart of God where the soul properly belongs. On the other hand, prosperity can become a severe temptation to which the believer may cling and from which he may draw life rather than the fountain of life (Psalm 36:9).

Life's circumstances are always in flux: "...facing plenty and hunger, abundance and need" (v. 12). Therefore, Paul is ever more diligent to finding contentment in the majestic Trinity through the means of grace (vv. 1-9). The soul that is heavenly bound through the Word, unceasing prayer, and ever-constant meditation will, like Paul, find strength for all things: "I can do all things through him who strengthens me" (v. 13).

Yet the life of a Christian is not defined by how many times a believer falls; rather, it's marked by how many times he rises from falling. A believer may fall seven times yet he will rise seven more (Proverbs 24:16). The soul will always be constantly tested, and at times, knocked off balance, challenged by the realities of this life. Falling down is indeed inevitable; however, through the means of grace, refocusing on true north and rising is destined. Some events may cause more turmoil for the soul than others; if that be the case, then to diligently seek God through prayer is of the utmost importance. Sometimes seeking him may only require thirty minutes, while other times he requires us to cry out night and day as Christ did in the garden of Gethsemane. Only by seeking God are we able to rise once again.

Concluding Thoughts

The soul of a gracious heart in the Lord's sight shines with a celestial brightness unrivaled by the stars themselves. The waves of turmoil and winds of chaos are always at work to dim and extinguish that light as much as is possible. However, the light of life within a believer is an eternal flame that can never be undone. The flame itself may sometimes burn brightly and be viewed from across the horizon; and at other times, it may be clouded by overcast skies, unable to be seen. The strength and proportions at which this flame burns is readily up to the believer. The stronger the foundation within the soul, the brighter the Christian's heart will burn with divine love. The stronger the flame the more stable the soul is in times of trial and testing, as the flame is the Spirit himself.

Spiritual stability of the soul is not achieved overnight. It is a process founded upon heart knowledge of God and the means of grace. The first time the disciples were tested with a *literal storm,* they fell utterly short and lacked the faith to endure it. Strengthing their ability for godly endurance was precisely the reason for the coming of the storm in the first place. Spiritual stability and maturity does not happen overnight, but through constant trials and consistent practice of the means of grace, it will certainly grow over time. The beginning of the Christian life will look more like the disciples as they first began, but as it progresses, it will begin to resemble more of Paul's or Christ himself. Paul also endured and went through similar storms, and astonishingly, he, like Christ, knew they were coming:

Since much time has passed, and the voyage was now dangerous because even the Fast was already over, Paul advised them, saying "Sirs, I perceive that the voyage will be with injury and much loss, not only of the cargo and the ship, but also of our lives." (Acts 27:9–10)

Sadly, no one heeded Paul's warning, and sure enough, the storm that he predicted came as predicted:

Since we were violently storm-tossed, they began the next day to jettison the cargo. And on the third day they threw the ship's tackle overboard with their own hands. When neither sun nor stars appeared for many days, and no small tempest lay on us, all hope of our being saved was at last abandoned. (Acts 27:18-20)

In spite of it all, Paul was steadfast in his faith, reassured by God that neither he nor any of the passengers aboard the ship would perish (vv. 21-26). This storm and the ensuing wreck was only one of many trials that Paul experienced in his lifetime (2 Corinthians 11:25). The longer one walks with God, the stronger and more steadfast will be the state of his soul. The foundational knowledge and practices outlined in this book, over the course of time, can and will produce a soul infused with the life of God and the strength of the Almighty:

Blessed is the man who trusts in the Lord, who trust is the Lord. He is like a tree planted by water, that sends out its roots by the stream, and does not fear when heat comes, for its leaves remain green, and is not anxious in the year of drought, for it does not cease to bear fruit. (Jeremiah 17:7–8)

It seems the strength of the church and of individual Christians has been in a steady decline over the years. My prayer is that the principles of this book will help to establish a stronger foundation in the lives of believers, so that one day a stronger generation may rise up and spark a spiritual revival.

Dear Heavenly Father, thank you for the gift of your eternal love which flows unto us through your dearly beloved Son. May the light within our hearts burn even brighter and our desire for communion and fellowship with you grow even more. Let rivers of life flow richly within our souls guiding us and pointing us toward a heavenly course. May the foundation which you have laid through the blood of your Son become even stronger in our hearts. Let our love for this world and the things of this world become a mere distant memory. Show us the depths of your heart that we may see Your beauty and, in turn, show the world who you are. Amen.

Endnotes

[1]   Jonathan Edwards, *Charity and Its Fruits*, in *Works of Jonathan Edwards, 8, Ethical Writings*, ed. Paul Ramsey (New Haven: Yale University Press, 1989), pp. 369-70.

[2]   Edwards, pp. 384.

[3]   John Owen, *Overcoming Sin and Temptation* (Wheaton, Ill.: Crossway, 2006).

[4]   Thomas Watson, *All Things for Good* (Carlisle, Penna.: The Banner of Truth Trust, 2011).

CPSIA information can be obtained at www.ICGtesting.com
Printed in the USA
LVOW11s0322211015

459078LV00001B/17/P